FIGHTING BACK

THE BLIZZARDS AND FLOODS IN THE RED RIVER VALLEY, 1996-97

The Forum
of Fargo-Moorhead

The setting sun casts a palette of color across floodwaters south of Fargo. 4A

Facing page: He's not horsing around. Lonnie Halverson and the Prairie Rose Carousel still stand after Wahpeton's Chahinkapa Park flooded. Ice clinging to the horse in front of Halverson shows how close the water came to the carousel. 5A

Compiled by the staff of *The Forum*
Story by Christopher Sprung
Forum photos by Colburn Hvidston III, Bruce Crummy, David Wallis, Nick Carlson and Andy Blenkush
Aerial photos by Larry Mayer of *The Billings* (Mont.) *Gazette*
Graphics by Dawn Brehm and Rob Beer
Editorial cartoon by Steve Stark
Edited by Terry DeVine

© 1997 Forum Communications Company
101 5th Street North
Fargo, ND 58102
Published by *The Forum*
William C. Marcil, Publisher
Joseph Dill, Editor

ISBN 1-56037-126-9

Front cover: Their appetite for homes never satisfied, floodwaters swallow another neighborhood south of Fargo. FC-1 (LARRY MAYER)

Back cover: President Bill Clinton offers his support to Grand Forks Mayor Pat Owens after she spoke at a briefing with the president and city officials at the Grand Forks Air Force Base. BC-1 (DAVE WALLIS)

Page 1: Residents of Georgetown find floating around town easier than walking or driving. Tony Wamback, above, floats his 3-year-old son, Nick, a quarter of a mile down Main Street to Tony's parents. 1A (ANDY BLENKUSH)

Pages 2-3: First the flood, then the fire. The remains of the Security Building in Grand Forks after a devastating fire demolished much of the flooded city center. This photo, taken two days after the fire, looks down Third Street North from First Avenue North. 2-3A (COLBURN HVIDSTON III)

Cover design by Dawn Brehm
Coordinated by *The Billings Gazette*
Printed by Fenske Printing Inc., Billings, Montana

CONTENTS

FOREWORD

Ironically, the entire *Forum* staff was together when the historic winter began. It was November 16, 1996, and we were enjoying our annual anniversary party at a motel in celebration of our newspaper's 118th birthday. A crippling blizzard sent us home early. Little did we know it had just begun.

Eight blizzards and smaller storms dumped more than nine feet of snow on the Red River Valley of the North, the most in state history. The snow began melting in March and sent the Red and other rivers into what became a record 500-year flood.

But we started discussing this book long before snow melted into floodwaters. Our photographers were out every day for months, producing eye-catching pictures as blizzard followed blizzard and the snow pile grew to awesome heights. Readers were calling as early as February, urging us to reprint the snow photos in a special section or supplement.

Inevitably, there were some deaths during this harrowing five months; damage to Red River Valley people and businesses will reach $2 billion. But we didn't want this book to be a recitation of disaster. We wanted it to show determined people fighting the elements. We wanted it to show volunteers helping people they would never meet by filling sandbags and building dikes, making sandwiches, taking strangers into their homes, donating cash and clothing, driving payloaders and bulldozers.

We wanted to show courageous police officers rescuing stranded people; organizations from the U.S. Marines to a Hutterite community helping out. We wanted to show people—some of them volunteers from 100 miles away—laboring without sleep day and night to fend off an unrelenting river; to show our people's sense of humor with signs like "unbottled water—free," tacked to a tree above the swirling floodwaters.

This book is that story, a historic record of our worst winter and spring.

I'm proud of the way our photographers and reporters covered this story which seemed to have no end; I'm proud of the color reproduction generated by our camera plate and press staffs.

I'm proud of the way the people of the Red River Valley fought the good fight. We dedicate this book to them.

We will express our heartfelt sorrow to victims of the blizzards and floods by donating to them through charities the after-expense revenue of this book.

The pictures in *Fighting Back* show the best of people at the worst of times. The indomitable spirit of our people—helped immeasurably by food, clothing and donations from all over America—allow us to prevail.

William C. Marcil
Publisher, *The Forum*
President, Forum Communications Company

Facing page: Hundreds of volunteers respond to an urgent, last-minute call to dike the Greenfields neighborhood in south Fargo as overland flooding comes rolling across the prairie. 6A ANDY BLENKUSH

Jerry Waller shovels a mountain of snow from the top of his Dilworth home so the roof won't collapse under its weight. 10A

ANDY BLENKUSH

Above: The Red River surrounds and lays siege to a farmhouse south of Fargo. 11A

Pages 8-9: Dawn uncovered yet more snow-removal chores for homeowners across the region, including Dave Odden of West Fargo. Odden clears some of the new snow that pushed the Fargo-Moorhead area's season total over 116 inches. 8-9A BRUCE CRUMMY

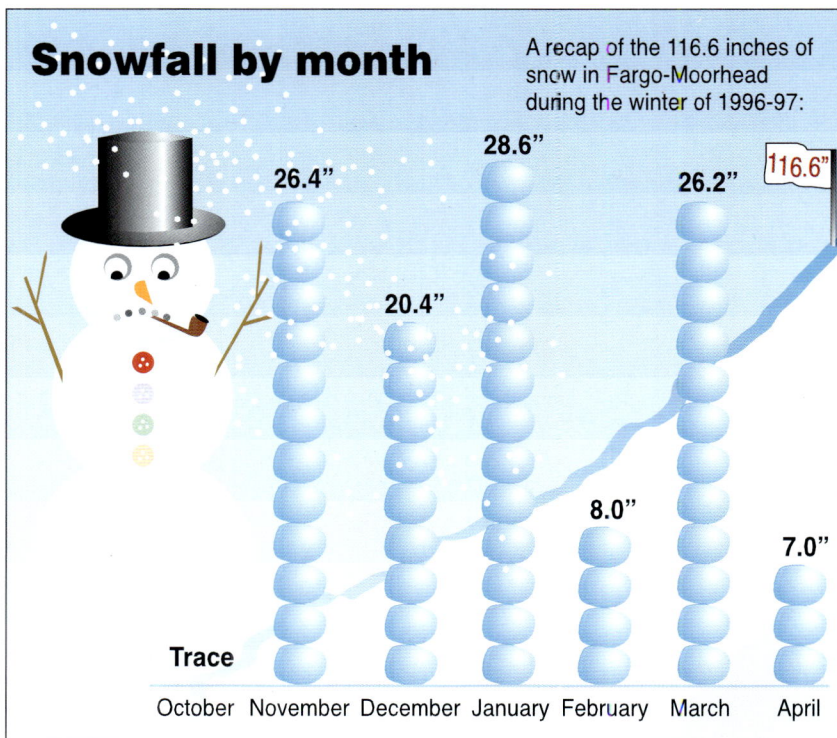

Snowfall by month

A recap of the 116.6 inches of snow in Fargo-Moorhead during the winter of 1996-97:

26.4"

28.6"

116.6"

20.4"

26.2"

8.0"

7.0"

Trace

October November December January February March April

ROB BEER / The Forum

Between Hell and High Water

Above: It's all part of the job. Alexa Hiebler used snowshoes to work her way to the wall of a Fargo residence on the 3200 block of South University Drive, where the Northern States Power Co. employee takes a meter reading. 13A

Facing page: Floodwaters made their way through one south Fargo neighborhood after another. 12A LARRY MAYER

The confluence of the Red and Wild Rice rivers south of Fargo. 14-15A

"THE RIVER GLIDETH AT HIS OWN SWEET WILL."

–William Wordsworth, *Composed Upon Westminster Bridge*

Trace your finger along a map or photo of the fickle Red River of the North and you will find it staggers side-to-side through the Valley in a drunken gait of curves and cuts and switchbacks as though it is somehow bewildered by its own course, unsure of its own direction, unable to make up its mind.

Or it may be that the river's path is more defiant than daft, a simple stubborn refusal to be marched quickly and efficiently from its beginning to its end. (Who among us would be different?) Nature dictates that it travel north from its birthplace near Wahpeton-Breckenridge to its resting place in Manitoba's Lake Winnipeg. The Red must bow to that decree but it makes the trip on its own terms and in its own time. It wanders east and west and east again. It backtracks south, lollygagging for about 545 river miles through a Valley that is only 315 miles from end to end. It loiters like a panhandler in cities and towns, idles in fields and near farmsteads.

For weeks the swollen Red stood center stage in a drama that would surround and swallow many of those places, and it played the role of cold villain and contemptible knave with skill and relish. It ground down the flesh and bone and spirit of its victims before it plundered their homes, their treasure and—at times—their hope. And when it seemed the Red had done its worst, it heaped mockery upon sore trial and delivered yet another blow.

But far more than a central figure in the record snows and floods that tormented the Red River Valley and the surrounding region, the river is an uncanny symbol of how those trying days unfolded.

Just as the Red defies the landscape, the seasons defied the calendar, refusing to pass in the orderly, straight-lined fashion set out by that dreary, predictable grid of days and weeks and months that adorns refrigerators and desk blotters and rules the lives of reasonable folk. Winter was a boorish and ungracious guest who arrived too soon, demanded too much and stayed too long. Spring kept its expectant hosts waiting without apology.

The Valley's story of deep snow and deep water takes as many twists and turns and switchbacks as the river itself.

And it all began with a relentless wall of white...

Kenny Jaeger tries to dig out his car from a snowdrift that accumulated during a blizzard. Freezing rain, snow and low visibility made travel in the Fargo-Moorhead all but impossible, and police ordered all non-emergency travel suspended. 16A ANDY BLENKUSH

"Winter tames man, woman and beast"–William Shakespeare, *Love's Labours Lost*

THE WINTER OF OUR DISCONTENT

Winter did not step gently onto the stubble fields of the Red River Valley. There were no picture postcard days where the umber skeletons of barren trees stood grand and lovely, magically transformed like Cinderella in a royal gown of glinting hoarfrost and snowflake lace. There were no Terry Redlin images of farmsteads snuggled like contented, sleeping cats in a downy quilt of snow, windows aglow with warm lamplight and a chimney puffing satisfied smoke.

No, winter stomped and kicked its way into the heartland. Its waffled heel and steel toe came down hard on the head of the Valley in a mugging that began in late October with a four-day rain that saturated the ground before freeze up. The beating would continue unabated for month after merciless month and it would subdue even the hardiest of souls.

November 15 marked the first punch, a light jab, just two inches of slush. It was followed the next day by a stinging combination of snow and raking winds that gusted near 50 mph. The two-day blizzard dumped 13.5 inches on the region.

A National Weather Service meteorologist in Grand Forks dubbed it a "classic blizzard, a classic winter storm for the Red River Valley. I'm sure we'll probably do it again sometime this winter," he said. At the same time, the forecaster downplayed the conventional wisdom and coffee shop theories that suggested the region was entering into what might be its worst winter in decades.

"A lot of people were talking ahead of time that this year was going to be a snowy and cold winter," he said. "Some people in this office have been suggesting that. And the climate gurus out in Washington, that was their prediction. This doesn't prove anything because if it all of a sudden turns mild, people are going to forget this."

The words would become one of those unfortunate arrows that not only misses its mark, but boomerangs and lodges squarely in the haunch of its archer.

Just days later, on November 20, a second storm added 6.1 inches of snow and a crust of freezing rain. Deep cold preserved the snowpack until mid-Decem

16

A south Fargo neighborhood is a maze of nicely sculpted snow piles resembling loaves of bread in this bird's-eye view of a January scene. 17A

OCTOBER 26-29
2.17 inches of rain saturates the ground before freeze-up

NOVEMBER 15
First snowfall yields just 2 inches of slush.

NOVEMBER 16-17
First blizzard arrives with 13.5 inches of snow and winds gusting to 47 mph.

NOVEMBER 20
Backed by winds of 15 mph, a winter storm drops freezing rain and 6.1 inches of snow. Consistent cold in late November through early December preserves the snowpack.

DECEMBER 16-18
Second blizzard rails for three days packing winds of 40 mph and 8.4 inches of snow. All of North Dakota remains under blizzard warning.

DECEMBER 20-23
Two quick winter storms produce near-blizzard conditions, pelting the Valley with 25 mph winds and 8.4 inches of snow.

DECEMBER 25
High of 14 degrees below zero, low of 27 below.

DECEMBER 31
Unexpected winter storm socks an isolated portion of the southern Valley. It leaves no new snow but packs raking winds up to 54 mph and wind chills of 50 below zero.

JANUARY 2
Unusually mild day posts daytime highs of 41 degrees.

JANUARY 4-5
Enormous blizzard drops freezing rain and 10.7 inches of snow in the Fargo-Moorhead area. Other areas received as much as 2 feet of snow. Winds ranged from 20 to 30 mph.

ber, when a succession of blizzards and storms—two of which lasted multiple days—kept the region hunkered down through New Year's Eve.

With January's arrival, it grew clear that winter intended, by slow degrees, to swaddle its victims in a heavy, white shroud and bury them alive. Four blizzards and one plain old ugly snowstorm (The difference lies in duration and wind) heaped just more than 2 feet of misery on Fargo-Moorhead and more in areas within and outside the Valley.

Moorhead city crews struggle against the snow and winds of the season's final blizzard to block off roadways fallen victim to the Red River. The Third Street underpass along the Red and under the NP Avenue bridge is one of the first to be blocked off by warning signs and barricades. 18A

The worst of that month-long buffeting took place the weekend of January 4-5, when freezing rain and nearly 11 inches of snow fell in Fargo-Moorhead—and more than double that piled up in areas south of the Valley.

Just two endless weeks into 1997, Wheaton, Minnesota, Mayor Wayne Hervey succinctly voiced the lament of an entire region. "It's been a damn long year," he said. "All 13 days of it."

Hervey suffered greatly at the hands of winter. A New Year's Day fire forced him from his home and chewed open his roof. Three days later, 27 inches of snow took up residence inside, ruining what belongings survived the blaze. His dilemma was cruel but not uncommon. Hardship was growing as abundant and widely strewn as the snow itself.

At its easiest, life had become a dreary exercise in snow-removal. Neighborhoods awoke and fell asleep to the sounds of shovels scraping pavement and the stuttering engines of four-cycle snow throwers. Plumes and arcs of white danced everywhere as neighbor heaped snow upon neighbor.

Cities and counties and townships exhausted men and machines and budgets to open roads that the wind folded closed again as soon as the plow wasn't looking.

"Every time they had a road cleared, they'd quit and five minutes later [it] would be filled back in," complained Foster County Sheriff John Statema.

The task was as futile as trying to cut a path through water. It simply was not possible to keep up. City streets grew as narrow and rutted as cow trails, and even the most traveled rural roads disappeared for days at a time. Cleared routes looked more like a system of tunnels than roads as mountainous berms stacked up on either side.

Snow dunes sweeping 10 and 20 feet high and sprawling for an eighth of a mile or more stood as common and forbidding on the prairie landscape as the pyramids in the Egyptian desert.

Arctic Bedouins clad in Carhartt coveralls, Red Ball boots and wool caps with earflaps struggled desperately to haul feed across the frozen expanse to ranging cattle, only to find some of the herd had wandered from the pasture across fence lines long since buried. Others would be found stiff and lifeless.

By mid-January, thousands of head were dead or dying. The state's congressional delegation called the winter "a full-blown crisis for North Dakota ranchers."

The region's dairy farmers struggled as well. When tanker trucks were hamstrung by impassable roads, milk didn't go to market on schedule. Holsteins, however, still produced it on schedule, and some farmers had no choice but to purge storage tanks and pump thousands of gallons of milk onto the snow, turning their yards into lumpy seas of vanilla ice cream.

Dejected barns and buildings everywhere sagged and collapsed beneath the burden of winter. The cavernous North Dakota Winter Show building in Valley City crumpled like an empty Grain Belt can when

A bicycle built for snow. A stalwart cyclist pedals past NDSU's Old Main after one of many winter storms. 19A

CHRONOLOGY

JANUARY 9-11
The new year's second blizzard brings 7.5 inches of snow and winds of 40 to 50 mph. North and South Dakota are declared federal disaster areas.

JANUARY 15-16
Winds up to 50 mph spawn yet another blizzard, though only a trace to an inch of new snow is added to the pile. Minnesota is declared a federal disaster area.

JANUARY 22
The fourth blizzard in two weeks slams into the region with winds up to 45 mph and 2 inches of new snow. Afternoon temperatures fell 30 degrees in 24 hours. By now, some drifts are 20 feet high.

JANUARY 24
A winter storm adds another 4.7 inches, bringing the season's total to 74.5 inches and surpassing the total snowfall for the previous winter.

JANUARY 26
Temperature falls to 30 degrees below zero, the coldest of the winter.

JANUARY 31
Quick moving weather front raises temperature to 41 degrees at 3 a.m. Few witness the thaw because the temperature fell back below freezing before 6 a.m.

FEBRUARY
Just 8 inches of snow falls all month, and there are no blizzards.

MARCH 3-4
Blizzard socks the region with 15.7 inches of the white stuff, bringing the total seasonal snowfall to 99.1 inches. That sets the record. The snow depth on the ground also reached a record 32 inches.

MARCH 13
A winter storm heaps another 6.5 inches onto the whole mess.

19

James McBenge takes an early-morning walk near a huge snowdrift in West Fargo, shielding his face from strong north winds and January temperatures in the minus teens. McBenge passes the McDonald's golden arches, peeking above at right, on his way to a convenience store. *20-21A*

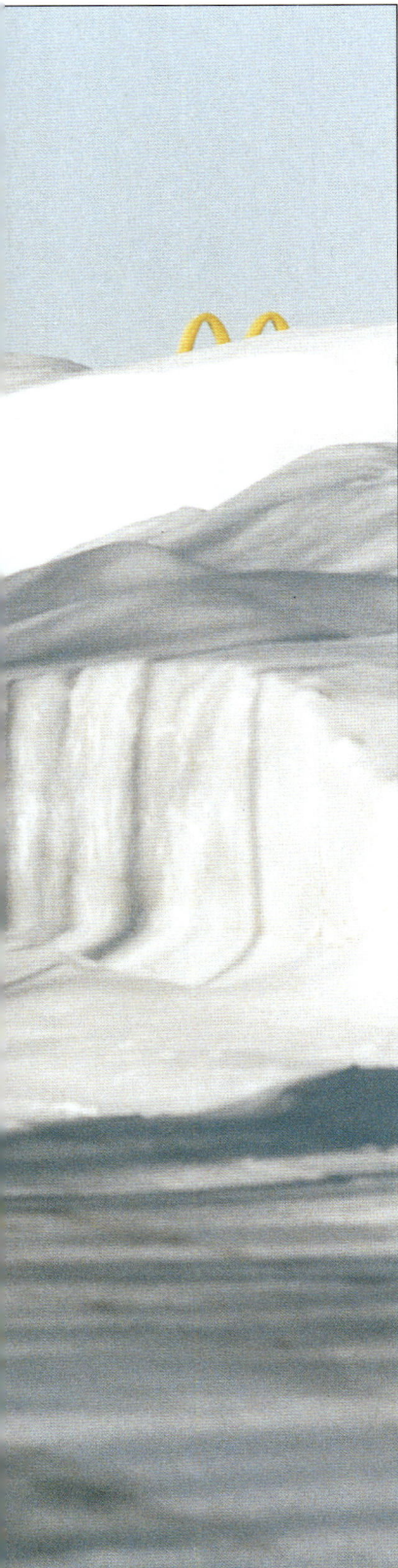

snow overpowered its curved steel roof and sides. The flat roof of a Fargo furniture store fell like so many jigsaw puzzle pieces onto the unsuspecting chairs, tables and sofas below.

Folks regularly scaled the icy slopes of hip, gambrel and gable roofs to clear clogged sewer vent stacks and shovel and rake—and snowblow—the weight from their creaking rafters.

Retail trade—with the possible exception of shovels, ice chippers, car batteries, snow throwers and other such survival tools—plummeted like the Great Wallendas in a stiff wind. No one could get out to shop. And when they did, sometimes there was little to buy. Delivery trucks could fall days behind in the back-to-back blizzards, making it difficult for small-town grocery stores to keep basics like milk, bread and eggs on the shelves.

Other supplies fell short as well. Road salt. Blood. Patience. But not everyone was frazzled and frayed.

Students greeted each and every blustery white-out with true rejoicing. Blizzards, after all, were school vacations fallen from blessed heaven itself. If historians one day trace a religious resurgence to this time, it no doubt will have its root in the prayers of kids who daily thanked God that they spent so much of the school year wrapped in a blanket on the sofa, munching Coco Puffs and staring mesmerized at morning cartoons.

It was barely mid-January and the winter already ranked 10th on the Valley's list of the all-time worst. North Dakota, Minnesota and South Dakota were declared federal disaster areas. The National Guard charged in with massive snow-moving machines to help fight the cold war.

By January 24, the 74.5 inches amassed in the Fargo-Moorhead area had surpassed the prior year's total snowfall. Many saw it as an ill-natured omen of things to come.

"We get the majority of our snow in the middle of January through March," observed Dennis Walaker, operations manager for the city of Fargo. "When you get this much snowpack already, it's not a question of whether the river will flood this spring but what the level of the river will be."

February brought some respite, just 8 inches of snow all month and no storms. But March came in like a pride of lions with fangs bared. An early blizzard and a winter storm mid-month pushed the season's snowfall well past the 100-inch mark, a record which stood for a century.

By now, people had come to want that record as a matter of hardy Midwestern pride. The more snow, the better. Pile it on. They wanted—no, they *needed*—an acknowledgment inked indelibly into the history books that they had indeed survived an ordeal without precedent. They had endured winter's worst and thrown it back one shovel at a time into the old man's face.

But there would be a price for that record. Tom Kubela could see it written large on the landscape of his family's farm near Wahpeton. As he gazed out the shop window at fields suffocating in snow, he knew they would soon be drowning.

"Everything out there that is white is gonna be blue in about four weeks."

The Sheyenne River overtakes Interstate 29 near Harwood. 22A

LARRY MAYER

ANDY BLENKUSH

Spring runoff overflowed choked ditches and surged across hundreds of county and township roads. Patricia Brandt, 41, and her 17-year old daughter, Monica, died after their pickup and horse trailer plunged into this washed-out section of LaMoure County Road 35 in predawn darkness. 23A

BRUCE CRUMMY

Fargo City Operations Manager Dennis Walaker wears his resume on his jacket. The city's famous flood fighter blocks noise from earth-moving equipment hustling to repair a breach in the Second Street North dike protecting downtown. The seeping dike was one of the biggest crises of the flood, causing city officials to order a second but smaller dike built behind it as a contingency. 23B

APRIL 4

The Red River Valley gets a cold, wet slap in the face as rain begins to fall in the afternoon. Crest projections are raised half a foot in Wahpeton-Breckenridge and Fargo-Moorhead. Between 50 and 100 county and township roads are washed out by overland flooding in northwestern Minnesota. Several homes near Sabin are in peril as the Buffalo River gorges the area.

APRIL 5

The Red River surpasses its record crest at Wahpeton-Breckenridge. Dikes break, flooding a seven-block residential area in Wahpeton; Breckenridge puts out a call for evacuation. Freezing rain and winds up to 50 mph bring down power lines and snap off power poles throughout the valley. Sandbaggers work in bone-chilling cold as the Red rises more than 3 feet in 24 hours in Fargo-Moorhead.

APRIL 6

Eight-year-old Jesse Maas dies in an early-morning mobile home fire in Lisbon. His mother and three siblings are hospitalized. Firefighters had difficulty reaching the house during a driving blizzard that hammered the Valley with 7 inches of snow.

Sandbagging takes a back seat to snowplowing. Power outages are widespread as winds up to of 70 mph snap poles like Tinkertoys. Wahpeton and Breckenridge wage a knock-down, drag-out fight with Mother Nature as 2.6 inches of rain combined with tree-toppling ice and heavy snow threatened the towns at the same time the Red is cresting at a record 19.2 feet.

DAVE WALLIS

Above: Unrestrained by high banks or hills, the river runs roughshod over the Red River Valley. 24A

Right: Volunteers in Cass and Clay counties donated roughly 60,000 hours in the first three weeks of the flood fight, not including the time hundreds of college students gave at all hours to fill and stack sandbags. The flood center opened April 1 in Fargo Civic Memorial Auditorium lobby with staff members Paulette Orth on the left, Mary Kenna, Mary Bourdon, Carol Schmidt and April Schwandt. 24B

"I come from haunts of coot and hern,
I make a sudden sally,
And sparkle out among the fern,
To bicker down a valley."
–Alfred Lord Tennyson, *The Brook*

LITTLE RIVER, NO VALLEY

E ven the most admiring eyes are underwhelmed by the physical stature of the Red River. More of a bloated creek than an honest-to-goodness river, to view the Red in its normal state is to watch a skinny garter snake wind its way almost undetected across the prairie.

It is a benign and friendly little serpent whose channel width ranges from just 200 to 500 feet. At its widest, the Red could almost be contained within the playing field at Tiger Stadium in Detroit, where the distance between home plate and the center field wall is 440 feet.

And at least four times in the past 65 years the river actually stopped flowing in Fargo-Moorhead and other places.

So, how does such a meek little stream manage to swell 10 miles wide as it did between Trail and Norman counties in mid-April, or 25 miles wide, as it did near Winnipeg?

The answer lies beneath your feet.

The Red River Valley is many things. It is a provider whose rich black fields fill the bellies of a nation and a world. It is a teacher whose many colleges and universities make it an epicenter of higher learning. It is an inviting and pastoral home to a patchwork quilt of farms and towns and cities all stitched together and spread comfortably across its plain.

But what it is *not*, is a valley.

Though it bears the name, what is called the Red River Valley is actually the dried up bed of Lake Agassiz, an ancient glacial lake carved eons ago by a slow-moving natural bulldozer known as the late Wisconsinian ice sheet.

As the glacier retreated to the northeast, water from melting ice and other sources filled the shallow basin it left behind. For about 4,500 years, Agassiz roamed across much of Manitoba, Ontario and parts of Saskatchewan. Only its index finger dipped down into North Dakota and Minnesota, the fingertip barely scratching South Dakota.

When at last the massive lake dried up, it unveiled the fertile Red River Valley, 17,000 square miles, every last one of them as flat as Frankenstein's head.

From the headwaters of the Red River outside Wahpeton-Breckenridge to its end point in Lake Winnipeg, there is but a subtle drop in elevation–just 233 feet over a distance of 545 river miles–and the Valley slopes just as slightly from its sides to its center.

Because the water is as sluggish as a southern drawl, the Red has never managed to cut much of a groove into the earth. It averages just 10 to 30 feet deep.

That mortar-board flatness and shallow channel are essential to creating the slow, sprawling floods unique to the region. With no valley or high banks to contain the river, rising water takes unfettered range on the plain.

At the same time, snowmelt pooling in the fields can move just as freely from section line to section line across land to meet the spreading river.

Of course, heavy rains can both prompt and worsen flooding. But over time, most of the basin's trouble with high water has been the result of melting snow.

Even so, heavy snowpack does not guarantee a severe spring flood if the melt is slow and the soil beneath is parched enough to drink in the runoff.

Unfortunately, that was not the case as the winter of '96 dissolved into the spring of '97. The ground was already choked and spitting up before the snows dwindled.

APRIL 7

Minnesota Army National Guard troops secure the towns of Ada and Breckenridge. The entire population of Ada moves out like war-ravaged refugees as the Marsh and Wild Rice rivers spill into town. The last straw for many was when pressure blew out drain plugs and basements filled with sewage. Ice chunks, remnants of the weekend storm, float in flooded streets. The last of more than 300 people are evacuated from Breckenridge.

APRIL 8

Hundreds of school children join the sandbag brigades as the Red continues to rise past 33 feet in Fargo-Moorhead. The Minnesota Army National Guard keeps a close watch on Ada, allowing only those with emergency business into the still-flooded town. An army of linemen scrambles to bring power back to the region, but many are left without power for the fourth day. Residents along the rising Sheyenne River watch and wait as their dikes hold.

25

DAVE WALLIS

Above: Thousands of sandbags line both sides of South River Road in Fargo near Lindenwood Park as they wait to be transported to the nearby permanent earthen dike already in place along the Red River. Each pallet contains 60 to 70 sandbags. 27A

Facing page: Overland flooding envelopes a south Fargo neighborhood. 26A LARRY MAYER

APRIL 9
The bodies of a pregnant Pamela Jean Wagner and her 3-year-old daughter, Victoria, are found face down in a stubble field a half-mile east of Kent, Minn. Their car plunged into the flood swollen Whiskey Creek. They survived the crash but died of exposure trying to walk for help. "She just walked and fell to the ground," said Wilkin County Sheriff Tom Matejka. "Couldn't make it any more, I guess." The National Weather Service hikes Fargo-Moorhead's crest prediction by one foot, sending sandbaggers scrambling to bring dikes to unprecedented levels. Floodwaters threaten Oakport Township north of Moorhead from two directions. In every direction, thousands shiver through their fifth or sixth day without electricity. Towns along U.S. Highway 75 north of Moorhead begin preparing for the worst.

APRIL 10
Fargo-Moorhead breathes a sigh of relief when it is discovered that the 39.5 foot crest prediction was based on a faulty automated gauge near Hickson. The sandbagging effort continues, but not with the same urgency of a day earlier. Some who showed up at Fargo's Volunteer Center are sent home. Some residents of Ada are allowed back into town, where they see sheets of ice resembling huge chunks of peanut brittle in heaps along boulevards.

> "It may be that the gulfs will wash us down."
> –Alfred Lord Tennyson, *Ulysses*

DEEP SNOW, DEEP WATER, DEEP TROUBLE

By the beginning of April, to fly over the Red River Valley was to witness the stunning return of extinct Lake Agassiz.

The melt which had begun slowly just 10 days prior was hastened in late March by temperatures that pushed into the 40s and 50s.

And as the snow retreated in defeat, an army of water rose up in its place and would soon lay siege.

ANDY BLENKUSH

Harwood residents shovel record snow out of the ditch to make room for the record water flowing past. 28A

"My deputies say they think they can take a Jet Ski and run all the way to Moorhead on farm land," observed Mahnomen County Sheriff Dick Rooney.

The same was true everywhere there was flat land. So it is no surprise that the first battles in the flood of '97 were fought not against the Red and its tributaries but against charging spring runoff.

At first, waves lapped at the edges of roads that had come to resemble causeways spanning a shimmering arctic gulf. Then engorged drainage ditches, too clogged with ice and snow to hold the runoff, became rivers themselves and roiled with whitewater. And when at last the water had risen high enough to cross the grid of roads damming it back, it began its march.

Rivers may be brutal in their conquest, but they tend to wage a methodical, set piece war. To great degree, their advance can be predicted, their strength calculated. Rivers declare their intent to invade days before they actually take the land beyond their banks. You may not be able to stop it, but at least you know its coming.

Overland water is far less noble an adversary. It is a sneaking guerrilla terrorist who preys on the unsuspecting, and attacks without reason or warning.

Only words beginning with the letter *w* seemed adequate to describe the overland onslaught. "It builds up behind a ditch and then– *Whoosh!*–it breaks loose and goes," recounted Sherwood Monroe, Dickey County's emergency coordinator. Enderlin Mayor Ed Morrow put it this way: "We thought we were all ready and then– *Wham!*– there it was."

Some of the areas hard-hit had never experienced flooding at all, let alone water of the magnitude that now rushed them. "There's no way we could have prepared for this," lamented Adrian Kiefer as overland waters coursed through Casselton. "I've seen it come up as much as a foot in 20 minutes…I pray to God it stops pretty soon."

Meanwhile, the work of building dikes along the Red and its tributaries continued at a fevered pitch. Most cities had begun their efforts around Easter, well in advance of the rising waters. By now a series of

Sean Finneman, with hip boots on his shoulder, walks in to aid his friend, Jamie Paquin, on submerged Clay County 52 south of Sabin. Finneman later learned that Paquin lost his home to the waters of the overflowing Buffalo River. 29A

Stan Baumann, a foreman for Northern Improvement Co. in Fargo, trudges through the mud and muck, taking elevations for a hurriedly constructed dike to save the Greenfields addition. 29B

APRIL 11
The Red appears to be cresting locally at the second-highest level in history at 37.55 feet. But Fargo-Moorhead residents dare not let their spirits soar. The great sea of Maple, Sheyenne, Wild Rice and Red backwater pooling around the metro area, combined with snow that must eventually melt, could combine for a second crest. Vice President Al Gore visits the Valley and lets people know that "you are not in this alone."

APRIL 12
The Red reaches an unofficial crest of 37.61 feet in Fargo-Moorhead. N.D. Gov. Ed Schafer tours Fargo and praises the community for binding together to fight the flood. Now the river's rate of decline will depend on the amount of precipitation and the rate of runoff from fields. The flood forecast for Grand Forks is at 49.0 the week of April 21.

APRIL 13
Although the Red drops two-tenths of a foot, Fargo-Moorhead residents are urged to stay vigilant for at least the next week. The river is not going to drop quickly. Upstream at Wahpeton-Breckenridge, a second crest is expected soon. Floodwaters break through a dike protecting Nora Lutheran Church near Gardner.

The northeast corner of Dilworth buzzes with activity as overland flooding from spring runoff endangers several homes in the community. 30A

earthen and sandbag levees was largely in place up and down the Valley. Just the same, a growing sense of urgency gripped city officials. The Red was rising uncomfortably high at its headwaters. And the sky had taken on a sullen, ominous glare.

By Friday, April 4, a sheer curtain of rain had been drawn across and beyond the Valley. Hundreds of county and township roads were overtopped or washed out in Wilkin, Norman, Clay and Cass counties alone as new spasms of overland flooding bedeviled the region. In Fargo, the river rose more than 3 feet in an hour.

The rain beat down steadily on Saturday as well–a total of 2.6 inches in all–and it critically weakened defenses in Wahpeton and Breckenridge.

"We're in the hurt bag," Wahpeton Mayor Dan Rood confessed as a seven-block area north of downtown was inundated. "We're drowning internally…If the rain would quit we could catch up but it hasn't let up at all."

Across the swollen river in Breckenridge, the trouble was much deeper. It had been eight years to the day that the Red reached its previous record crest of 17.95 feet. By 8 o'clock that Saturday evening, the river stood at 18.14 feet and rising. Alarmed city officials declared a state of emergency.

By midnight, water the color of three-day-old tea coursed 2 and 3 feet deep through the streets.

"We're losing dikes all over town," despaired Jack Thompson, the city's emergency service coordinator. "We've lost it."

Struggling to keep their footing in the rushing water, police clad in chest waders slogged door-to-door trying to move people from their homes. In time, hundreds would flee.

Amidst that tumult and panic, fate heaped trial upon trial as a grudge-bearing winter returned one last time to humble the Valley and a great many beyond.

NICK CARLSON

Unexpected rising water sent sandbaggers scrambling to save several homes on the north side of Amenia. Mary Blixt reacts to the water surrounding her Amenia home. 31A

DAVE WALLIS

Ranell Hatch, left, and Joe Berg, working for Master Construction, carefully wade through chilly water to get to a telephone switching facility in Casselton. The men were careful to stay on an approach road to the building because the water was about 6 feet deep. 31B

APRIL 14
Relief turns to frustration as a second faulty river gauge forces Fargo to abandon automated number reading. The Red is on the rise again here. Breckenridge evacuates 200-300 homes after overland flooding pours more water into the city. The town of Davenport calls in dike workers after a rural dike break near Kindred sends water its way. The towns of Hendrum and Perley fight back whitecaps against their dikes. Damage estimates to the region's electrical transmission system are estimated at $30 million following the season's brutal final blizzard and ice storm.

APRIL 15
The Red keeps rising, topping the 38-foot mark, and it looks like it will crest for the second time this week in Fargo-Moorhead, threatening the 100-year-old record of 39.1. In Breckenridge, hundreds more are forced from their homes as overland flooding from the Bois de Sioux River hits town. The Red is 10 miles wide along the Traill-Norman County line.

APRIL 16
Floodwaters from the Sheyenne River overflow into the Wild Rice River and make a run for the southwest corner of Fargo, threatening six housing developments and Interstate 29. The Red keeps rising in Fargo-Moorhead, hitting 39 feet just before midnight. Iced-over farm fields in the Valley are liquefying and running off. Grand Forks residents don't like what they see to the south.

Wind and ice teamed up to snap utility poles off at the base between Fargo and Casselton during the final blizzard. 32-33A

"Tis a fearful thing in winter
To be shattered in the blast,
And to hear the rattling trumpet thunder
Cut away the mast."
–James Thomas Fields, *Ballad of the Tempest*

AN ILL WIND BLOWS

The temperature fell as steadily as the rain that Saturday and by evening all of creation was encased in a thick chrysalis of ice.

Trees that had nobly weathered half a century of nature's cruelest insult bowed and shattered beneath the weight of their new translucent armor.

A 2,000-foot television broadcast tower near Galesburg, crashed to the prairie like slain Goliath. Thousands of wooden power poles that once stood as rigid and stalwart as Marine sentries were laid low, their spines snapped and rudely splintered.

In the predawn hours of Sunday, April 6, the season's eighth blizzard–the 13th winter storm in all–clawed its way across North Dakota and tore into the heart of the Red River Valley with lavish fury.

Winds packing gusts of 70 mph blinded the region with 7 inches of new snow, pushing the season's total to 116.6 inches–or 9.7 feet–in the Fargo-Moorhead metro area alone.

Electric and telephone lines fell to the ground in a frozen snarl. One by one, cities and farmsteads and towns fizzled and flickered into darkness like bulbs on a faulty string of Christmas lights. An estimated 85,000 people in the Valley and beyond would face the cold for days without electricity.

When the power failed, so did the pumps and sewer lift stations that kept some of those cities and towns and farmsteads ahead of the rising water. While the blizzard raged, desperate struggles would begin.

In Lisbon, exhausted firefighters scrambled to patrol dikes, man gas-powered pumps, and move elderly residents from their heatless homes as the Sheyenne River rose to a record high. Paralyzed by the raking snow and wind, they were powerless against the early-morning homefire that killed an 8-year-old boy and sent his family to the hospital.

APRIL 17
Just after midnight, the Red surpasses its all-time high mark in Fargo-Moorhead. City leaders go on radio at 12:30 a.m. to warn residents of two far-south developments to be prepared to evacuate. The Red surges to 39.51. A section of dike blows out on Fargo's South Terrace Drive, sending a wall of water into Oak Grove Lutheran School and the surrounding neighborhood. All but a few residents of Fargo's Southwood Drive neighborhood are forced to leave their homes.

APRIL 18
The Red is out of control in Grand Forks and East Grand Forks. Residents of both cities are told to evacuate. By evening, water has spilled into downtown Grand Forks. The river is closing in on 53 feet. In Fargo, the city makes a tough call to build a massive dike on the far south side to hold back overland flooding from the south and west. The Red is cresting at a record 39.55 feet in F-M.

APRIL 19
The disaster worsens in Grand Forks. Hours after the overflowing Red surges through the city, fires race along some downtown rooftops. Firefighters are helpless in streets up to 4 feet deep in water. In Fargo, while the city's new dike is going up, residents to the south and thousands of volunteers work around the clock to save their homes from the onslaught of overland flooding. They get some relief when Cass County removes a section of Highway 81.

33

As would happen to many other rural residents, winter's violent return forced Ken Nelson from his farm near Halstad.

"Up until the snowstorm and power outages we were holding our own," he said. But by Sunday night, the temperature in the house had fallen to 40 degrees and floodwater was 4 feet deep in the basement.

Nelson and his wife were able to warm themselves in the cab of their idling pickup, but it proved an inadequate incubator for the shivering Black Angus calf they brought in with them. The newborn animal died.

The season's final blizzard was especially cruel to livestock. Already weakened and stressed by months of hardship, as many as 50,000 head of cattle perished in North Dakota alone during that single storm. Total losses for the state over the winter and spring were estimated at 120,000.

"When you picked up a calf you were carrying almost a 20-pound chunk of ice," one farmer recounted. "We were drying them off with heat lamps until our electricity went out."

Meanwhile, in Ada, the city's destiny had been eerily spelled out on the marquee of the Orpheum Theater. "TURBULENCE," it said in big block letters. "SECOND SHOW."

On the blizzard's heels, breakout water from the Marsh and Wild Rice rivers charged through the city, turning streets into churning canals. Basements filled as water cascaded in through windows and erupted in geysers through floor drains.

Hundreds of people were helpless against the water, but perhaps none more so than the Rev. Mark Widman. Stranded in Grand Forks, he listened by telephone as his wife, Kara, struggled.

"My wife and children were in a cold house and it was dark, and it was my daughter's birthday, and I couldn't be there," he recounted days later in voice trembling with frustration. "My wife was trying to drag everything out of the basement and she had two crying kids."

By Monday, April 7, aluminum fishing boats and mammoth National Guard transports maneuvered their way around the ice floes adrift on the arctic sea that Ada had become. Passing residents hand-to-hand from their porches to the waiting trucks, troops evacu-

DAVE WALLIS

APRIL 20
The Grand Forks fires are under control, but only after 10 historic downtown buildings have been destroyed. About 75 percent of Grand Forks and all of East Grand Forks have been evacuated. Many go to shelters at the Grand Forks Air Force Base and in communities up and down the valley; others move in with friends or relatives. In Fargo, the massive sandbagging efforts on the far south side save most of the endangered homes.

APRIL 21
Grand Forks begins the grim task of demolishing burned-out brick buildings downtown. A crane sitting in 5 feet of floodwater begins taking swings at the historic structures. Water is receding in Fargo-Moorhead. South of Fargo, township roads that have been covered by water begin popping into sight.

APRIL 22
President Clinton visits Grand Forks, touring the area by helicopter and speaking with evacuees at the Air Force Base. He pledges $488 million in flood aid to the Dakotas and Minnesota. The Red crests at 54.1 in Grand Forks, more than 5 feet above the previous record. In Fargo-Moorhead, thoughts turn to cleanup efforts as the Red drops below 38 feet.

ated most of Ada's 1,700 residents and closed off the city. No one would be allowed back in for days.

The picture was equally grim in Breckenridge, where 400 homes were evacuated. The 3 feet of water in the streets had thickened to a mortar of slush and then hardened, cementing cars and trucks and heavy equipment fast to the ground. The Red had frozen the fleeing city in its tracks.

Cold tightened its grip and the Valley was again transported back in time. Overland water that just two weeks prior had given terrible rebirth to Lake Agassiz was now transformed to a glacial sheet. Mile after infinite square mile had become a vast wind-

Above: Water overflows the banks of the Maple River and covers a road while isolating two outbuildings on a farm north of Enderlin. 34-35A

Upper Left: Once-flooded streets turned to frozen slush and trapped vehicles like this car in front of the Breckenridge Post Office. 34A

Mike Johnson holds empty bags over the spout and Mike Vad shovels sand as the two fill sandbags in Breckenridge. Using a home-made bag filler made from a sheet of plywood and two plastic traffic cones with a section of the tops cut off, six people can fill 100 bags in about 11 minutes. The two men themselves filled 350 bags in about two hours. 36A

polished mirror reflecting back at the sky.

It would be a week or more before many cities and farmsteads knew the comfort of electricity and heat and running water. Armed with huge portable generators, the Guard set up emergency shelters in churches and schools. But many would test their survival skills and try to stay in their homes.

Roger Miller used his gas barbecue grill to warm one room in his Perley home. "You take the lava rocks out, burn it for an hour with the window open, and shut it off. It works pretty well," he said. With no running water, Miller melted snow to fill his toilet tank. He cooked on a camp stove, read by lanterns and entertained himself with a 5-inch, battery-operated television.

At Chris Malakowski's house in Shelly, a gas oven provided heat and heavy extension cords snaked through the house and under the front door, carrying precious electricity from a gas-powered generator outside to the vital appliances—a refrigerator and a lamp.

It was tolerable, she said. "But the waterbed does get a little brisk, I must admit." Her family kept its sanity on the dark and chilly nights by playing cards and board games.

"Monopoly, we play a lot of Monopoly," chimed in daughter Megan. The water and electric utilities must have taken on new meaning during those games. "And the railroads," Malakowski joked. "We could get out of town."

Many people would not be satisfied to merely "Take a Ride on the Reading." Lured by the promise of clean clothes and hot showers and cable television, they left their homes for shelters or hotel rooms or the spare beds of relatives with electricity to share.

"You try to wait it out," observed Dale Tellinghuisen. "But next thing you know, you're living off roasted peanuts and melted snow before you realize this isn't any good and you've got to get out of here."

The Valley's final blizzard may have tamed man and woman and beast, but it did not tame the Red. The river continued to rise. And as it did, an unprecedented army of volunteers came to greet it.

LARRY MAYER

A ring and a prayer. Homes became islands encircled by protective sandbag dikes like this one near Hickson. 37A

APRIL 23

Classes resume for Oak Grove High School students at Concordia College in Moorhead. Meanwhile, the Oak Grove school cleanup begins with help from faculty and students from Hillcrest Lutheran Academy in Fergus Falls. Cleanup efforts intensify in Ada, where most of the town's 1,700 residents have returned. It'll be awhile until that happens in Grand Forks and East Grand Forks, where some homes are still flooded to the rooftops and others have been pushed off their foundations.

APRIL 24

Some Grand Forks families are allowed back to fetch belongings and look over the damage for a few painful hours. They're struck by the force of the floodwater and the stench left in its wake. In Breckenridge, life might never really get back to normal, but many of the 3,750 residents are cleaning up and searching for some sense of normalcy.

APRIL 25

Fargo is slowly returning to normal as National Guard and city crews begin taking chunks out of the 40th Avenue South dike and city officials start making cleanup plans. Meanwhile, the folks in Pembina, North Dakota's oldest community, wage the state's last battle as the raging Red's floodwaters move toward Canada.

Dozens of Casselton students form a line to pass sandbags as they build a dike along the north side of the school. Many other students were busy working at bag-filling stations and other diking sites on the north side of the city. *38A*

> "To be nameless in worthy deeds exceeds an infamous history."
> —Sir Thomas Browne, *Urn-Burial*

THE KINDNESS OF STRANGERS

Morrie Lanning trudged along the rutted crown of a dike separating an anxious Moorhead neighborhood from the writhing serpent that aimed to swallow it whole. He scoured every contour of the clay bulwark for cracks, leaks, even the subtlest trace of weakness. But what the city's mayor saw that day was the very essence of strength.

There, watching over the mechanical health of a vital sewer lift station, stood a man whose only companions for nearly a day and a half were the wind, the cold and the rising water. "He was there for 31 hours straight by the time I got there and was hoping to be relieved by 7 that night, which would have been a 36-hour stint," Lanning recalls. "He was a little punchy to say the least."

This was not one of those times when a worker could at least console himself with the money he would earn on his miserable watch. The man wasn't working for overtime or double-time rates. He wouldn't collect a fat check for his trouble. He was a volunteer. Lanning didn't know his name, didn't even know if he lived in Moorhead. All the mayor knew is that he felt indebted to the man.

In that same way, flood stricken victims up and down the Red River Valley are beholden to thousands of nameless, faceless people who answered their desperate pleas for help.

High school and college students abandoned desks and textbooks and turned out in droves to fill and heave sandbags. They were inexhaustible machines that needed only periodic refueling with gut-bomb burgers and Dairy Queens and chocolate and Mountain Dew.

The pistons of their arms and legs churned for hours without fail. Their backs never once succumbed to the creeks and cramps of their thirty- through seventy-something counterparts. And they brought to the lines an infectious playfulness and sense of humor.

On Monkey Island, a small enclave of houses on Hillsboro's northern edge, high school students took a running start and leapt the 4,000-sandbag ring dike they'd just finished building around Glenn Brustad's home. Once airborne they'd seize the coarse braid of rope hanging from a nearby tree and swing out to taunt the waters less than a foot from the dike.

The school was very clear about the rules: Only students age 14 and older would be excused for sandbag duty. And yet Brustad's yard and those of his neighbors were filled with 13-year-olds.

"Don't tell our moms," begged one girl who was on the losing end of a wres-

APRIL 26
The Red is down below 36 feet in Fargo-Moorhead. The worst is over here. Engineers' calculations and crisis management helped Fargo, Moorhead, West Fargo and Dilworth fend off wholesale flooding like that in Ada, Breckenridge, Grand Forks and East Grand Forks. In Fargo, floodwater damaged 86 homes, or one-half of 1 percent. In Moorhead, floodwater entered 41 homes. Initial estimates put financial damage in Grand Forks-East Grand Forks at $775 million.

APRIL 27
Grand Forks residents flock back to their neighborhoods. Security is loosened. It's been 10 days since the Red flooded their city. Officials seem to understand how important it is for people to get back. Some residents even move back in despite having no tap water or sewer service.

APRIL 28
Good riddance. That's what Valley residents are feeling as the Red River's crest— miles and miles of muddy, greasy water laden with sewage and farm runoff—passes through Pembina into Canada. Its departure signals the end to the area's worst flood in history.

APRIL 29
Disasters bring out the best in people. Today a woman who did not want to be identified pledged to give $2,000 to each household in Grand Forks and East Grand Forks. That's $15 million. Later, the benefactress was identified as Joan Kroc, widow of Ray Kroc, founder of McDonald's fast food restaurants. Some folks are donating one can of soup to the Salvation Army and Red Cross. All of the help is welcome.

Volunteers use broomsticks to push sand into bags below during dike building efforts in Fargo's Oak Grove neighborhood. The volunteers worked in the rain before a blizzard struck later that night. 40A BRUCE CRUMMY

tling match with a sandbag that outweighed her by a good 20 pounds. "We…well…we lied to come here, OK?"

As students in Casselton fought back overland flooding that swamped their city, one boy jokingly asked his teacher: "Are we going to get better grades for this?"

"We'll have to wait and see about that," the teacher replied. "Is it making you smarter?"

Chuong Dinh had already learned his lesson and was putting it to practice in a south Fargo neighborhood one night. At 16 years old, Chuong knew well the value of an outstretched hand. Born in Vietnam, he came to Fargo in 1993 with a sister—and without parents—after spending two and a half years in a Malaysian refugee camp.

Were it not for the kindness of strangers, Chuong would never have witnessed the flood of '97, and he certainly would not have become mired in the snowbank that now swallowed him to the hips.

His braced left leg paralyzed by polio, Chuong could not cross on the 2-by-4 balance-beam that spanned a 3-foot deep moat encircling a threatened house. Determined to join the sandbagging effort, he tried to cross a bridge of deep snow but his leg crashed through. An undercurrent of ice water filled his boot as he struggled to free himself using a garden spade as a crutch.

When at last he was on his feet, someone offered to drive the boy home. "Naaah. It's just water," Chuong said as he ambled toward the house. "These people got it a lot worse than me."

That sentiment is what brought Don (no last name, just Don) from his farm near Pelican Rapids to the sandbag lines nearly every day for a week and busloads of people just like him from dozens of cities throughout the region.

It's what brought scores of Hutterites from their spartan rural colonies to slog and sweat in the yards of homes far too luxurious for their own modest standards. Not only did the Hutterites give their labor, they brought pounds and pounds of smoked turkey and other treats to feed families and fellow volunteers.

LARRY MAYER

Water, water everywhere and not a drop to drink. A flood-stricken resident makes a desperate, thirsty plea south of Fargo. 41A

BRUCE CRUMMY

Blasted water hazards. Mayville-Portland-Clifford-Galesburg High School senior Ross Johnson searches the rising waters for a golf ball he and other friends hit into a low area at Second Avenue South and First Street in Mayville. 41B

APRIL 30
There's a chill in the air. It should be warmer than this on the last day of April. But it could be worse. Just take a look at the last 29 days.

MAY 15
Estimates reveal more than 16,000 homes in Grand Forks and 2,500 homes in East Grand Forks are damaged by floodwaters. Hundreds of businesses in both cities fell victim as well. Estimates for other cities emerged as well.
In Breckenridge, 600 homes—more than half of the city's residential structures—were damaged.
In Ada, between 200 and 300 homes suffered damage during the flood.

MAY 17
The Red finally drops below flood stage at the river's headwaters in Wahpeton-Breckenridge, where the disaster began.
The river was still more than 6 feet above flood stage in Grand Forks-East and Drayton; and 8 feet above in Pembina.

MAY 22
Farm losses for the winter and spring in North Dakota are tallied to stunning effect.
• More than one million inundated acres would go unplanted in the spring.
• About 123,000 cattle perished.
• 400,000 bushels of stored wheat and barley were lost.
• $8.1 million in machinery was damaged or destroyed.
• Losses for farmhouses and service buildings exceeded $27 million.

41

Sandbaggers make a valiant effort to save a majestic Fergus Falls home that had been moved to 42nd Avenue South in Fargo a few years ago and was partially restored. The home later fell victim to overland flooding. 42A

"They kept bringing stuff. Unreal," said Linda Bergh of Fargo. "They checked to make sure everything was OK before they went home in the evening. And I don't know who any of them are or where they are from."

And, ironically, the feeling that others had it worse than he did is what brought David to the sandbag line.

Well, the train brought him—from Chicago or Denver, depending on which time you asked him—in an empty boxcar.

A lumbering man in his 40s with a salt-and-pepper beard and a plum colored shiner over his left eye, David toiled long hours piling sandbags for people who would never be likely to invite him in.

In return, he accepted sandwiches offered by the Salvation Army—but not more than a couple. "That's all I can get in my stomach," he said. "It shrunk up. I never know when I'm gonna eat."

At night, David slept outside with his dog.

Like so many people, 8-year-old Andrew Frovarp would have given all that he had to ease the loss of another. After working to help save an elderly couple's south Moorhead home, he turned to his mother and sadly announced: "Mom, I wish it was our house that was flooding, not those old people's."

That is the beauty of a sandbag line. It may well be the most decent and egalitarian structure ever devised by human beings.

In that efficient meshwork of hands moving in an endless routine of grabbing and passing, grabbing and passing, each person is an important as the next. In

The dike surrounding Nora Lutheran Church near Gardner was unable to hold back encroaching water. Just hours after this photo was taken, the church was flooded. 43A

Water invades the streets of Ada. Most of the town was evacuated as the city fell victim to overland flooding from the Marsh and Wild Rice rivers. 44-45A

one motion you are the boss who forces work on another. In the next, you are the burdened.

Distinctions of race and class disappear on the sandbag line. And in those grueling hours there develops a rarefied air of agreement and focus and vision that human beings under other circumstances seem unable to summon and sustain.

A bag moves down the line from the hands of a banker to a fry cook to a teacher to a welfare mom to a firefighter to a deadbeat dad to a gangbanger to a farmer to a rabbi to a grocery store cashier to an accountant to a jail inmate to a bread truck driver to a cop to a drunk to some poor schmo who lost his own house to the flood two days ago. On and on through the social strata the bag travels hand to hand until it finds its place in the protective wall

There is no black or white or brown. There is no rich or poor. There is no regard for age. There is only the social class of the dirty and the tired. And everyone belongs.

"What tells me that we're going to survive is the many acts of camaraderie I've witnessed," Breckenridge Mayor Kal Michels observed at the height of his city's torment. "I saw people—whose own homes were flooded—out there helping to shore up dikes. We'll clean this up and be stronger for it."

More amazed by the strength of the Valley's volunteers than the scope of its destruction, President Bill Clinton would remark: "You have shown that when we think of our duties to one another, our own lives are better."

The stricken may never shake each and every anonymous hand that braced them in their battle against the water. They may never recognize all the mud-caked faces. But they will long remember the kindness of people whose names they never knew.

"Things which you don't hope happen more frequently than things which you do hope."
—Platus, *Mostellaria*

FALSE READINGS, FALSE SECURITY

By April 9, the Red was at 35.4 feet and rising quickly in Fargo-Moorhead. On that day the National Weather Service raised its crest prediction to 39.5 feet—a foot higher than expected and well more than it took to submerge all but a tiny portion of the two cities in the great flood of 1897, a drowning that had gone unsurpassed for a century.

The announcement shot panic through Fargo-Moorhead and every downstream community along the Red and its tributaries. Even Noah wasn't prepared for water like that. Already bone tired, city crews and homeowners up and down the Valley began a frenetic race to build up their dikes.

The warm wind that spun off the Valley the next day in the form of a collective sigh of relief may well have spawned a tornado in Oklahoma. It turned out that the Weather Service's prediction was wrong. A faulty automated gauge near Hickson had produced an inaccurate reading.

A couple days later, the Red would reach an unofficial crest in Fargo-Moorhead of 37.61 feet, the second-highest on record.

"There are a lot of people feeling good right now. I hope that feeling continues for a few more days until we're out of danger," said Dennis Walaker, Fargo's chief flood fighter.

Though the water was expected to rise again upstream in Wahpeton-Breckenridge, Walaker downplayed any impact on Fargo-Moorhead. "As far as this second crest, boy, all I see is a slowing in the (drop) of the river."

Another automated gauge would agree—and be wrong. The Red was still climbing. To make matters worse, the glacier left by the blizzard and subsequent cold snap was melting away and overland flooding again bedeviled the region.

By April 15, the engorged Bois de Sioux River made a cross-country run from its banks and hell broke loose a second time in Breckenridge. A tor-

rent bowled through the city's south side, immersing cars and homes in as much as 12 feet of water.

Several hundred more Breckenridge residents would be evacuated from their homes. Mayor Kal Michels nearly wept as he watched Coast Guard rescuers move elderly residents from their apartments. "They've seen the dust bowl and the Great Depression," he said. "They understand adversity, but this is hard."

Farther north, a second battlefront cracked wide open in Fargo as breakout water from the Sheyenne

Already distressed and starving after a miserable winter, herds of deer up and down the Valley searched in vain for forage and dry land. 46-47A

and Wild Rice rivers began a deep-water assault on hundreds of homes in the city's southwest corner.

"I don't know if we can keep it up," lamented Fargo Mayor Bruce Furness. "We don't have enough resources to handle all these hot spots. They're either going to have to stop happening or we're going to have to decide where we're going to go."

The clock and the calendar had just barely acknowledged April 17 when the Red River surpassed its century-old high of 39.1 feet and moved into the

record books. "That false forecast saved our butts as far as I'm concerned," Moorhead City Manager Jim Antonen later acknowledged. "It was a godsend. It turned out to be closer to the truth than anyone imagined. Thank God we added two more feet to our dikes."

By day's end it would climb to 39.51 feet and crush a neighborhood while getting there.

No one knows for sure how it happened, but a weakened dike protecting a home along South Ter-

A visibly tired and distressed Dennis Walaker, Fargo's operations manager, surveys the Oak Grove neighborhood after a dike break caused Oak Grove Lutheran High School and several homes to be lost to the record-breaking flooding Red. 48A

A student slogs his way through thigh-high water that flooded the Oak Grove Lutheran High School campus after a sandbag dike at a nearby home failed and allowed the Red River to pour into the neighborhood. 48B

race Drive gave way to the river's relentless pressure. The Red blasted like Emmitt Smith through the hole in that defensive line and went on an open-field tear toward a second dike that protected the campus of Oak Grove Lutheran High School.

The brigade of students and teachers and volunteers working to fortify the sandbag structure watched in horror as Emmitt charged in for a touchdown.

"A 5-foot wall of water knocked the dike right out from under us," senior Paul Thureen told his friend Aaron Clemens. "We're lucky we're alive, Clemens. We're lucky we're alive."

Every building on the campus would be engulfed in 4 feet of water and filth and 25 homes swamped. Dejected sandbaggers walked away. There was nothing left to save.

"The Oak Grove campus is history," said Dennis Walaker. "There's no plan left anymore other than to get everybody out of their areas."

Besides, there were more pressing battles now. Fifty square miles of water was barreling overland toward Fargo from the south. If not contained the water could fatten the Red and cause city-wide destruction.

A massive earthen dike on the city's southern edge from West Fargo to the river could hold the water back, but the price of safety would be the possible sacrifice of more than 550 homes isolated on the wrong side. City leaders agonized. Ultimately, the needs of the many outweighed the needs of the few. They would build the wall. And if need be they would close it.

Residents on the unprotected side appealed to the court of last resort. "Tell people to pray," one woman said. "We need heavy artillery."

It would not be the first time that flood fighters in Fargo-Moorhead and throughout the Valley wished that the burden of leadership belonged to another.

NICK CARLSON

Bags on the ground and under their eyes. Sandbagging goes into the night after the dike broke in the Oak Grove neighborhood. 49A

Ella Ambuehl, 91, is one of the last Ada residents to be evacuated from her home by Minnesota National Guardsmen. 50A

Minnesota National Guard troops take a rare and deserved rest in a makeshift bunkhouse in Ada. 51A

"One who never turned his back but marched breast forward; never doubted clouds would break; never dreamed, though right were worsted, wrong would triumph."
–Robert Browning, *Asolando*

OF LEADERS AND SUPERHEROES

Their eyes gave them away.
Lack of sleep had blackened and closed them to slits with the efficiency of a heavyweight's right hook. A mapwork of bloodshot lines forked and swelled and broke out each day like the rivers they fought back, until to meet their gaze was to view a spreading flood of red.

Those were the eyes of women and men who bore the worries and expectations of their cities and towns, of their friends and neighbors.

Lending every conceivable skill, they were engineers and planners, machine operators and laborers, mayors and city managers. They were firefighters and cops and rescue workers. They were secretaries and soldiers. They were volunteer coordinators and neighborhood block captains and a legion of others too numerous to list.

Week after week they devoted their muscle and their cunning to the Herculean task of trying to beat back and outwit cruel nature.

A newspaper profile of Dennis Walaker, Fargo's operations manager, was accompanied by a large cartoon depicting the man as an invincible comic book superhero.

It was an image projected onto many community leaders throughout the Valley, one they surely found more daunting than flattering. After all, a cape bestowed by an admiring public can just as readily be fashioned into a noose and used to lynch a superhero who proves all too human.

And those who stood at the front lines and directed the battle against the flood of '97 knew well they would be lauded only a moment if the crisis passed without harm, but ridiculed and second-guessed for decades if all of their efforts ended in watery failure.

Human shoulders were not built to bear such weight. Most would shrink from the task, but time and time again those who served rose to the occasion and carried their communities.

And they did it at the expense of their own families and property and at the sacrifice of their physical

The mood is tense and somber as Fargo Mayor Bruce Furness announces construction of a massive clay dike to be built roughly along 40th Avenue South from the western Sheyenne Diversion east to the Red River. Public Works Director Pat Zavoral points to the line of demarcation that effectively isolates 600 homes in new south Fargo neighborhoods from the rest of the city. 52A

and emotional well being.

They sustained themselves on a diet of prayer and adrenaline and coffee and cigarettes and anything that came cold and greasy from a paper or plastic bag and could be swallowed in three bites. Aspirin and antacid were always on the dessert cart.

Only occasionally were they nourished with kind words or gratitude.

Their beds—when they managed to find one—were makeshift heaps on office floors and chairs and truck cabs. They missed daily appointments with razors and toothbrushes and soap and water. They looked like hell and felt even worse.

As the flood neared its most critical stage in Fargo, Walaker rallied his exhausted troops. "I know everybody's tired," he said in a voice as rough and graveled as a township road. "We just have to keep going. There's a lot of people out there depending on us."

No doubt those same words were spoken many times in fire stations and city halls and emergency command centers up and down the Valley. And they were spoken to great effect.

When the days grew more difficult and trouble attacked on several fronts, trucks and bulldozers strained doubly hard to push up barricades.

As fast as insurgent waters broke free of river banks and raced cross-country, rescuers in helicopters and boats and Humvees plucked the stranded from their besieged homes and farmsteads. Soldiers brought heat and light and a ray of hope to scores of cities left dark and shivering.

Those designated superheroes kept their heads, as Rudyard Kipling put it, when all about were losing theirs. Voices of certainty in uncertain days, they allayed fears and buoyed sinking spirits.

When the water had done its worst, they comforted the victims and kicked themselves for falling short. With none to console them they sat alone, head in hands, and wondered what they might have done differently.

And when wounded by unjust criticism, they did not return insult in kind, but paid the price of leadership. They steeled their spines, as superheroes do, and pretended not to feel it.

But their eyes gave them away.

Above: Grand Forks Water Rescue Volunteers carry Matt Proulx to safety on Washington Avenue. Proulx and his grandfather, Frederick Fried, were trying to navigate too close to the treacherous currents near Lincoln Park in a small dinghy. 53A

Left: Minnesota Army National Guard members block the entrance into Ada from the south side through Highway 9 after most of the residents fled rushing floodwaters. 53B

All the world is a flood stage. The Red at various heights at Dike East near the midtown dam in Fargo. (Top to bottom): 54A, 54B, 54C

Craig Harrier of Bismarck loads supplies that will help his son-in-law, Doug Kuhn, fight floodwaters at his home north of West Fargo near the Sheyenne River. Kuhn went into Fargo to buy a second generator to power four sump pumps after word came that they were losing ground in their battle to save the home. Harrier and Kuhn walked the canoe through more than a mile of floodwaters to the residence. 55A

Above: Ada residents Linda Krippner and her 5-year-old daughter, Samantha, search through several boxes of donated clothing in the Borup school gym, a shelter for many of the Ada refugees evacuated from their homes. 58A

Right: Though not a trend likely to spread to New York and Paris, rubber boots and blue jeans were high fashion in flood-threatened areas of the Red River Valley. 58B

Pages 56-57: Shards of ice and sheets of water made navigating many stretches of road a treacherous adventure. 56-57A

Oh, say can you see that our house was still there? Sandbaggers at the Tim Doyle home in Oak Grove planted an American flag in the dike. 59A

Emily Roers guides one of her quarterhorses out of her residence along Wall Street north of Moorhead as Red River floodwaters cover the street. *60A*

ANDY BLENKUSH

Right: North Dakota Civil Air Patrol cadets, ranging in age from 12 to 18, help the North Terrace neighborhood in Fargo prepare for the forecast floods. Squadrons from Fargo and across North Dakota were on hand to help sandbag. 61A

Below: Paul Bjugstad is loaded on to a bus at the Veterans Administration Medical Center in north Fargo to go to a VA center in St. Cloud. The move was a precaution due to the flooding Red River near the medical center. 61B

NICK CARLSON

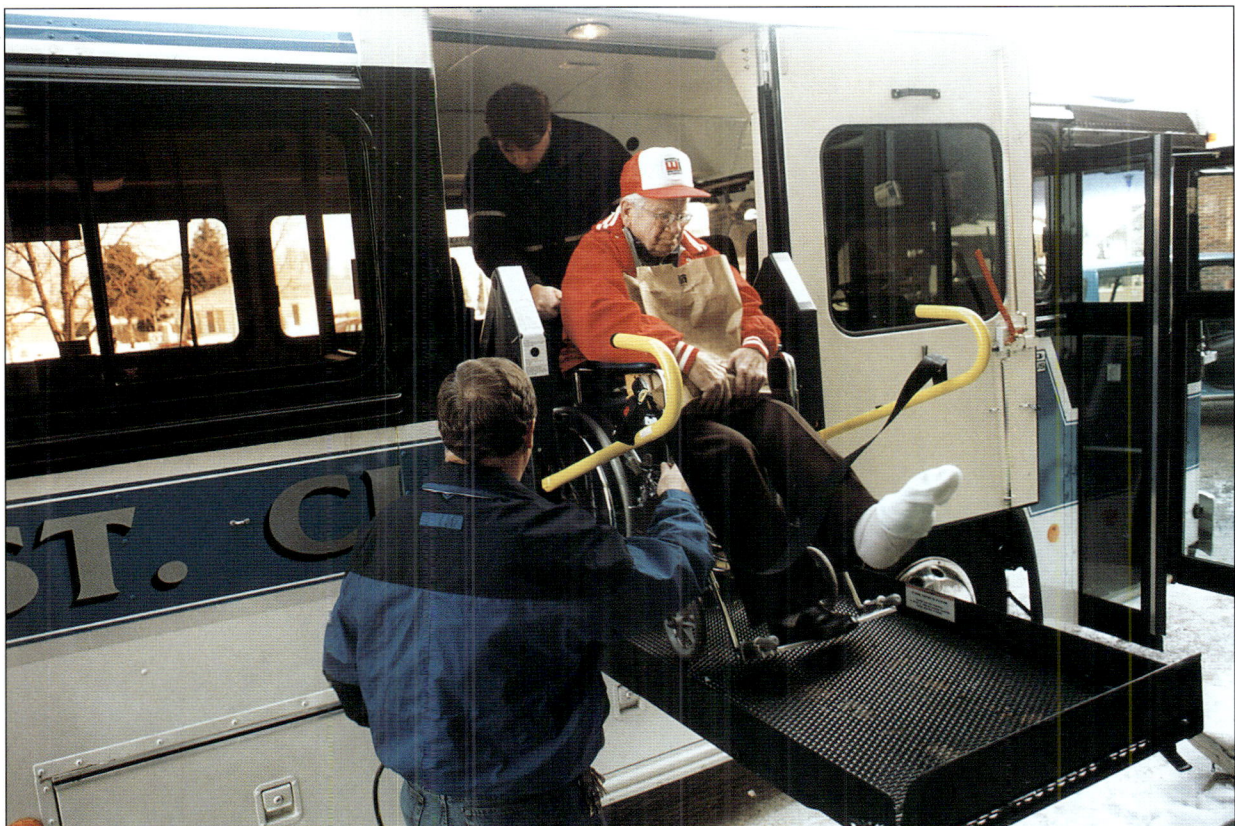

Steam rises from the ground as heavy equipment operators hastily build a dike in a field to protect the southern edge of Hendrum.
62-63A

Students and other volunteers in Hendrum fill sandbags in preparation for the flood-waters to come. 63A

With overland flooding threatening the northeast corner of Moorhead, residents were forced to clear several feet of snow to provide a base for a hastily erected sandbag dike. 63B

"You see, of course, if you're not a dunce,
How it went to pieces all at once.
All at once and nothing first,
Just as bubbles do when they burst."
  –Oliver Wendell Holmes, *The Deacon's Masterpiece*

HELL AND HIGH WATER

While Fargo scrambled to build its southern line of defense (which never required closing), the Red began a brutal siege of Grand Forks and East Grand Forks that would lay waste to the cities.

At 6 a.m. on Friday, April 18, warning sirens screamed the 3,000 residents of Grand Forks' Lincoln Drive neighborhood to their feet. "It jarred me out of bed," recalled Joann Hurley. "I thought it was the end of the world."

Water had bested the dike and was headed toward the low-lying neighborhood. Frenzied residents heaped belongings into cars and pickups and fled as the first of many forced evacuations got under way.

Hurley stood on a corner and stared in awe as water streamed past her house on Belmont Road, her lips repeating the same whispered words: "Holy Moses ... Holy Moses ... Holy Moses."

But Moses held sway over the Red Sea that no one would hold over the roiling Red River. By late night, the water had risen to near 53 feet and conquered dike after dike. So many were the breaches on both sides of the river that it was easier to count the places where the structures did not give way.

"That was my lowest day. The young engineers were coming in with tears in their eyes because the dikes were failing and the patches weren't working," recounted Grand Forks Mayor Pat Owens. "They thought it was their fault, all those people being forced from their homes."

It grew clear the damage could not be confined, and officials moved to empty both cities entirely.

"People can expect to see water running down the streets in front of their house in the morning," warned police Lt. Byron Sieber.

By Saturday, April 19, downtown Grand Forks stood 4 to 6 feet deep in the Red's chilly embrace,

COLBURN HVIDSTON III

Above: Floodwaters 3 to 4 feet deep turned Reeves Drive into a reflecting pool for this stately white house, a Grand Forks landmark. 65A

Left: Cruising through the intersection of Third and Demers, a Coast Guard skiff patrols the heart of downtown Grand Forks. 65B

Facing page: Houses separated from their foundations bob haplessly near the lower Lincoln Park area in Grand Forks shortly after the 54-foot crest. 64A

Demolition begins even before the devastation ends. A crane takes a wrecking block to the fire-ravaged ruins on 4th Street North in downtown Grand Forks between Demers and First Avenue. 66-67A

and residents fled in boats. In East Grand Forks, roof peaks bobbed like buoys on the water. "The retreat started on one end of town and went to the other," recalled East Grand Forks mayor Lynn Stauss. "People were frantic. It reminded me of Vietnam. Everything was happening at once. A bulge in the dike here. A bulge there. By two o'clock Saturday morning we lost the whole town." And the river continued to spread with the sure speed of vicious gossip or a filthy joke.

So much water everywhere. And not a drop of it would quench the blaze that started in the historic Security Building and spread in a rage to 10 other downtown buildings that Saturday night until the very heart of Grand Forks was reduced to rubble and ash.

Hampered by waist-deep currents, firefighters and National Guardsmen struggled in vain against the flames. "Our entire town is flooded and now our town is burning," Fire Battalion Chief Jerry Anderson said in frustration.

The noise was as inescapable as the river. Wailing sirens. Roaring water. Crackling fire. Bleating motorboats. The huff-huff-huff of military helicopters as they churned the air, hovering and darting like olive drab dragonflies. Ears ached with tragedy. Eyes watered with it. The fetid stench of sewage and fuel and filth was overpowering.

By Sunday, a veil of sepia-tone smoke draped a downtown that looked strangely like an ancient, hand-colored photograph. Its buildings stood in magnificent ruin, like sacked and smoldering Rome oddly misplaced among the canals of Venice. "I really didn't believe it would get to this proportion," said Lynae Sondreal. "This is something you only see in the movies."

Eventually, most of Grand Forks' 50,000 residents and all 5,800 in East Grand Forks would be forced to flee. "I'm just convinced this disaster will be the worst in our history," observed North Dakota Gov. Ed Schafer.

Acting on Weather Service predictions, the two doomed cities had prepared for a crest of 49 feet. That mark, however, would be raised several times in the five-day period before disaster visited, leaving little time to build up the system of levees.

Some blamed river forecasters for sealing the cities' watery fate. Others felt nothing could have restrained the rampage. "It all seems so futile now," sighed Betty Van Vugt as she sat on her porch and watched the water rise. "They could have built all the dikes in the world and I don't think it would have mattered."

The Red crested at 54.1 feet—more than 5 feet above its previous record—on April 22, the day President Clinton toured the shattered cities.

Clinton pledged $488 million in aid to the flood-stricken region. Then the commander in chief became consoler, telling evacuees at the Grand Forks Air Force Base: "You don't have to be ashamed if you're heartbroken."

With floodwaters pressing up to the top landing of her Bois de Sioux Mobile Estates home in south Breckenridge, resident Karen Boothby yells out to passing relief agency workers in a boat ferrying groceries April 16 to stranded homeowners. Floodwaters remained at high levels to this date and beyond following the first disastrous deluge the evening of April 5. *68A*

Right: Minnesota National Guardsmen ease motorists over wood ramps protecting large hoses that moved water to keep Clay County Road 93 open. The road was the only link to Oakport Township area homes. 69A

Below: Roads stand out as water floods the fields south of Davenport. 69B

Power lines and plumbing often were the only tethers that moored some Grand Forks and East Grand Forks houses to their foundations. 70A

More than 100 years in business were temporarily interrupted for Lyons Auto Supply in the Grand Forks city center. 70B

Two of three disabled loaders sit in chest-deep water in front of the administration building on the Oak Grove Lutheran High School campus. The machines stalled making a valiant effort to carry sandbags to an emergency levee after a neighborhood sandbag dike broke and flooded the area in Fargo. 70-71

Chris Welle looks from his deck near the Moorhead Country Club at the floodwater near his home. The dike broke early that morning sending water toward Welle's home. 72A

NICK CARLSON

CRAIG MCEWEN

Left: Paul Mergens carries Kent Hjelseth back to his house in the River Oaks development in south Moorhead. Hjelseth's home was protected by a dike surrounded by floodwaters. 73A

Below: Minnesota National Guardsmen prime one of about a dozen huge pumps to keep Clay County Highway 93 open, the last access to the Oakport Township area north of Moorhead. 73B

RAGING, RISING RED RIVER

FLOOD GAUGE	April 18, 1997 **39.55'**	April 6, 1897 **39.10'**	April 15, 1969 **37.34'**	April 9, 1989 **35.34'**	April 19, 1979 **34.93'**

FLOOD GAUGE
40'
39'
38'
37'
36'
35'
34'
33'
32'
31'
30'

1 2 3 4 5

Flood stage is 17'.

DAWN BREHM / The Forum

COLBURN HVIDSTON III

Above: Two residents of the Oak Grove area leave their home when one of the few major dike breaks in Fargo caused a neighborhood to flood. 74A

Facing page: Volunteers wade through chilly floodwater to carry sandbags from Fargo city utility trucks to the administration building at Oak Grove Lutheran High School after the campus flooded. 75A DAVE WALLIS

The floodwaters of the Red River bear down on Fargo's downtown area. *76-77A* NICK CARLSON

Vic Hurt explains to Governor Ed Schafer and first lady, Nancy, how his dike keeps his property dry on Forest River Road south of Fargo. The dike was constructed to accommodate the original crest forecast. When the crest was raised, he cut through his deck to raise the dike. 78A

Vice President Al Gore on the Second Street dike in downtown Fargo. 78B

John Lunday, left, and Jon Stainbrook try to patch leaks in the dike as water rolls into the basement of the Dave Pink residence at 129 S. Terrace, Fargo. *79A*

Red River Valley crest levels

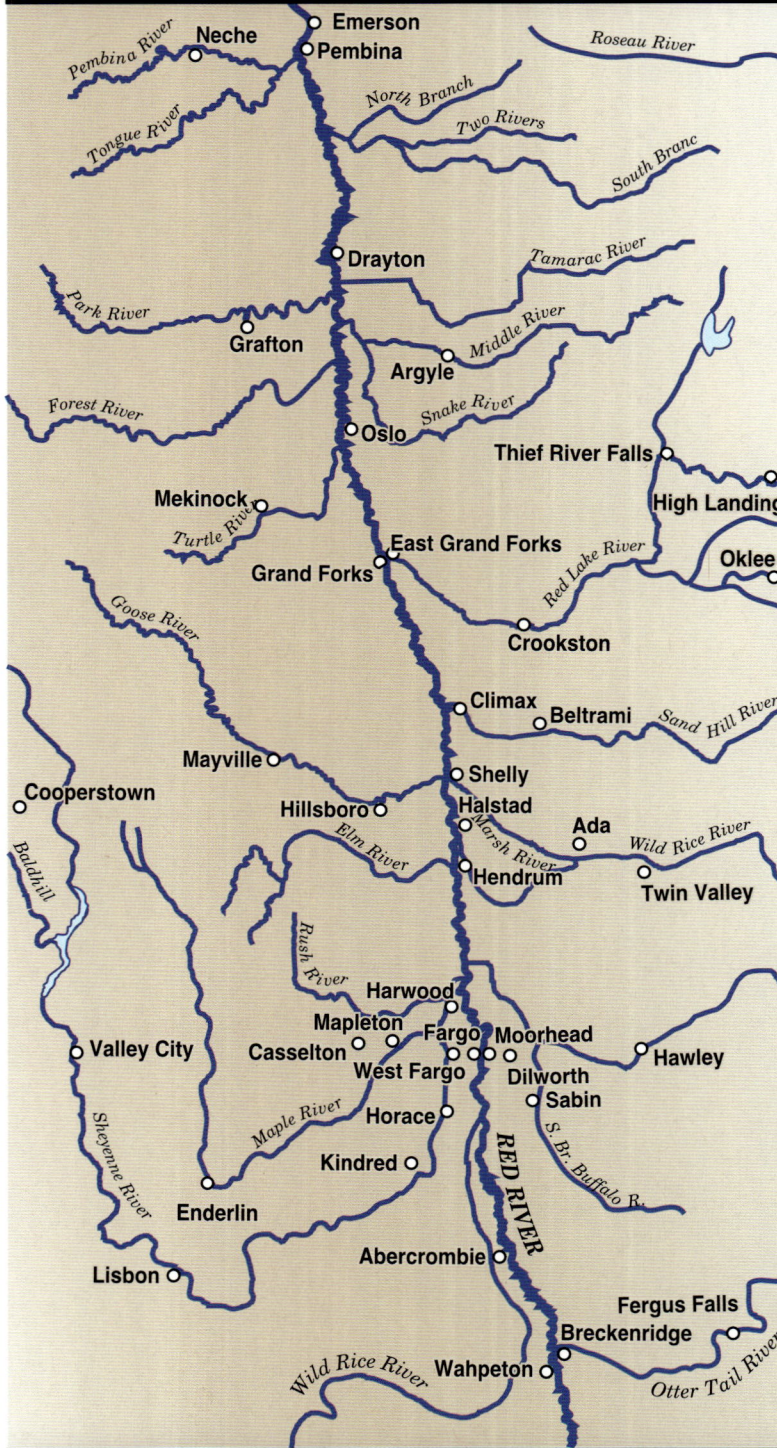

Unofficial record levels

River	crest	1997 Date	Record	Previous Date
Red River				
Wahpeton, N.D.	19.2	April 6	17.95	April 5, 1989
Fargo	39.5	April 18	39.1	April 6, 1897
Halstad, Minn.	40.8	April 19	39.0	April 22, 1979
East Grand Forks, Minn.	54.0	April 22	48.8	April 26, 1979
Drayton, N.D.	45.6	April 25	43.7	April 28, 1979
Pembina, N.D.	54.9	April 27	53.8	May 1, 1979
Sheyenne River				
Lisbon, N.D.	19.2	April 5	19.0	July 1, 1975
Kindred, N.D.	22.0	April 8	21.7	July 6, 1975
West Fargo	23.3	April 9	21.5	July 26, 1993
Harwood, N.D. (div.)	892.0	April 10	890.7	April 13, 1996
Maple River				
Mapleton, N.D.	15.5	April 4	15.0	July 2, 1975
Wild Rice River				
Twin Valley, N.D.	15.9	April 6	12.6	April 5, 1989
Hendrum, N.D.	33.7	April 19	32.3	April 21, 1979
Buffalo River				
Hawley, Minn.	10.7	April 8	10.4	July 18, 1993
Marsh River				
Shelly, Minn.	25.7	April 20	23.4	April 19, 1979
Red Lake River				
Crookston, Minn.	28.1	April 17	27.3	April 12, 1969
Wild Rice River				
Abercrombie, N.D.	26.5	April 6	24.6	April 11, 1969

Unofficial non-record levels

River	1997 crest	Date	Record	Date
Red River				
Oslo, Minn.	38.1	April 23	38.6	April 26, 1979
Sheyenne River				
Valley City, N.D.	18.7	April 19	18.9	April 25, 1979
Maple River				
Enderlin, N.D.	12.4	April 18	15.4	June 30, 1975
Buffalo River				
Sabin, Minn.	19.2	April 6	19.9	July 2, 1975
Dilworth	27.0	April 8	27.1	July 2, 1975
Red Lake River				
High Landing, Minn.	11.9	April 11	13.4	July 3, 1975

Floodplain characteristics

The flatness of the Red River Valley coupled with the river's slow-moving water and shallow channel are prime factors contributing to the area's slow, sprawling floods. There are few natural barriers to contain the water. Compare it to the Sheyenne River, whose narrow valley suffers shorter floods.

Red River

Sheyenne River

Source: "A River Runs North, Managing an International River" by Gene Krenz and Jay Leitch.

DAWN BREHM / The Forum

Left: Homes in low-lying areas like the 500 block of Lincoln Drive in Grand Forks were among the hardest hit. 81A

Below: Driven by a heavy current, a wooden barricade is the only thing moving through the ghostly, desolate center of Grand Forks' stricken downtown. 81B

Above: Iceberg in a nice burg. Linda Campbell pushes an ice chunk away from the dike protecting her home in the River Oaks addition in south Moorhead. 82A

Facing page: Dale Redmer uses a tractor and scoop to transport his daughter Corrie, 14, and son Cody, 11, home as he treads cautiously along washed-out 19th Avenue Northwest just west of Cass County Highway 17. Both children attend Park Christian School in Moorhead. Their school supplies, including his saxophone, are in the scoop at left. 83A

"I propose to fight it out on this line if it takes all summer."
–Ulysses S. Grant, *in a letter to Secretary of War Edwin M. Stanton*

RISING ABOVE THE WATER

Frieda Colman had seen the Red River grow surly so many times by now that it didn't scare her anymore.

"Old age takes care of a lot of fright," the 96-year-old woman observed as she calmly made sandwiches in her kitchen while the river stood outside her back porch hollering threats. "You take it as it comes."

And when it does, you don't back down. Ever.

That obnoxious little bully of a waterway had pushed a lot of folks around in the 30-some years that Frieda lived along Fargo's riverfront. A lot of them high-tailed when the river got mean. But the Red had never succeeded in running Frieda off. And it wasn't about to do it this time—even if it was more belligerent and wild than she had ever witnessed before.

Frieda wasn't going anywhere. Period. "My friends think I'm absolutely out of my mind to stay," she said. "I admit it. But I'm happy to be here."

This wasn't just about preserving walls and roof and a foundation. There was more at stake than that. Much, much more.

This was the place where she nurtured her family and her flowers and made them both bloom. The place where the gentle ghosts of a thousand memories sat beside her and kept her company on lonely evenings. The place with 5 acres of grass out front, every blade of which she still loved to cut and comb and style. The place that held her independence.

If the river wanted to take all that, it would have to get past Frieda. And before it reached her, it would have to subdue the massive 8-foot, 10,000-sandbag fortress that her grandsons, Craig and Brad Colman, and a slug of volunteers labored day and night to build.

"Now we are safe," she pronounced with confidence as she served ham and roast beef sandwiches to the men. Craig tried to tell her there was no guarantee but she refused to hear it. Not a word. You don't argue with Grandma.

"Just say 'Yes we are,'" she scolded.

But simply saying it wouldn't make it so. Not for Frieda or countless others in the Valley who fought

A tractor cuts through the road to the Jerome Fjelstad place so floodwaters from the Sheyenne River could keep moving southeast of Kindred. 84-85A

grueling battles to save their homes and farmhouses from the water.

They pinned their hopes on three things: the strength of their homemade levees, the stamina of their bailing pumps and the endurance of their hardy spirits.

The dikes were nothing less than avant-garde masterpieces of human ingenuity, strangely art-like sculptures of sandbags, plastic sheeting, plywood, suspended beams and studs. Of aluminum rain gutter, wire mesh, cinder block, PVC piping, and maybe a few discarded table legs and an old beer sign or two thrown in for style.

Engineers, who build by precise mathematical calculation of force and tolerance and load-bearing capacity, would look upon the backyard monstrosities in dumbstruck awe. They regarded the levees as new man-made wonders of the world. Not because they rivaled the likes of the Great Pyramids of Egypt or the Temple of Artemis at Ephesus. They simply made a man wonder how in the world the structures managed to stand at all, let alone when tested by the

tremendous force of stampeding water.

In the orchestra pit behind those levees, electric and gas-powered pumps played a flatulent symphony of chugging and gurgling and sputtering and belching as they drank gallons of seeping water and spit it back into the river.

People learned to hate that most unmusical melody. Their ears rang with the ceaseless din. Their heads throbbed and split. And yet the only thing that could sound worse...was silence.

That would mean the pumps weren't working, the house filling, the fight was lost. Silence was a dreadful thing indeed.

And so they kept constant vigil against the quiet and the rising water as sleepless day blurred into sleepless day.

"We have to take the water from the inside to put it on the outside to do it all over again," Rollie Johnson explained as the machines tended to their cycle of bailing at his home in Oakport Township. "I don't even know what I'm fighting for, except a little bit of pride."

Many of Johnson's neighbors fled the rural subdivision by boat after it was surrounded by floodwater. But a few diehards tried to tough it out and found creative ways to help each other along.

To keep his family in clean clothes, Greg Holland snaked the discharge hose of the washing machine through the dryer vent in the laundry room and over the protective dike. The washed duds then had to be shipped by canoe to the neighbor's house, where the dryer was still hooked up.

They were getting by, but Holland was beginning to understand the pressure that ground his neighbors into submission.

"A lot of people gave up the last two days," he said. "You can only take so much of it. Mental fatigue is what's taking them down hard...real hard."

The physical strain was equally brutal. It cut through every sinew and taxed the very bone and marrow of those who fought the water.

Harry Hawken felt its ache. The Fargo man hadn't slept in days for fear that the river would sneak past his dike the moment his eyes were closed. He kept his boots on and tried to doze on the kitchen carpet, but rest was as scarce as dry land.

"My back is so stiff I couldn't get off the floor. I had to roll over and had to crawl my way up," he said. "You can't close your hand anymore your fingers are so tired from grabbing a sandbag."

Many would withstand the physical and mental anguish to fall exhausted into their beds knowing they had bested the water. They would sleep the deep and glorious slumber of the saved.

Others would succumb to the water. Forced to flee, they would sleep in someone else's bed. Or in an Army cot. Or on a wrestling mat next to strangers on a gymnasium floor. Theirs would be the fitful sleep of the rescued and evacuated.

Heather Larsen kept the water away from her south Moorhead home until the river rose to 38 feet. Then "We got killed at the front of the house, not the back (where the river is)," she said. "We lost it at 4:10 on—what day is it today? Thursday?—we lost it at 4:10 Tuesday."

August Stuhrenberg surrendered his Breckenridge home as well. Six pumps and a gas generator were

Mike Edenborg and Julie Rodriguez move a mounted buck's head plus a board of mounted walleyes and other belongings in a canoe. The couple helped neighbor Wanda Lackmann move possessions to higher ground when floodwaters from the nearby Red River forced the evacuation of homes in the Town and Country Golf Course area in south Moorhead. 86A BRUCE CRUMMY

no match for the fast-moving overland floodwaters that swamped the city. "I couldn't keep ahead of it anymore," he said as he stepped from a boat to a dry stretch of pavement. Besides, "there's no fish in there."

Even the indomitable Frieda Colman—who stared that river down and dared it to cross her—would flinch. She decided to stay with family when the water rose too high. Frieda was lucky, though. Her home suffered only the slightest damage. A little soggy carpet. She would be back tending her flowers and grass in no time.

But multitudes up and down the Valley were not so fortunate. When the waters receded, they would come home to basements filled with sewage and filth, to warped doors and buckled floors and floating furniture. To a lifetime of memories washed away.

The pictures of weddings and graduations and naked kids in the tub with a dollop of suds on their heads. The love letters and diaries that still remembered kisses long forgotten. The favorite neckties and dresses, great-grandma's Bible. The baby's first shoes. Scrapbooks that chronicled lives from birth certificate to obituary. The only quilt that mom ever made.

The church organ. The teddy bear that had been a devoted companion for 20 years. All of it gone.

Clad in chest waders and rubber gloves they would gather the drowned artifacts and pile them 10 feet high on the boulevards to be hauled away with the fouled carpets and the decaying Sheetrock. And they tried to keep it in perspective as they prepared their memories for a pauper's burial in the dump. They still had what they cherished most. Each other.

"It's not the end of the world," said Tim Cameron as he assessed the damage in his Grand Forks home. "It just seemed like it for a day or so there."

Some would reclaim their homes in weeks. Others in months. And many like Mary Pat Fortier and her son Michael, would never go home again.

Fire reduced the Fortier's downtown Grand Forks apartment to a pile of blackened brick. "We did lose a lifetime," said Michael. "For us, there's no pumping out, there's no drying out or salvaging anything."

"We lost everything. My diamond watch, my diamond rings…"said Mary Pat, her voice trailing off. "I don't even have a pair of shoes. We've got nothing, absolutely nothing, do we, Mike?"

Concordia College student sandbagger volunteers Dallas Anderson, left, and Paul Marek rest on sandbags in the back of a pickup transporting them to their destination on South Rivershore Drive. 87A

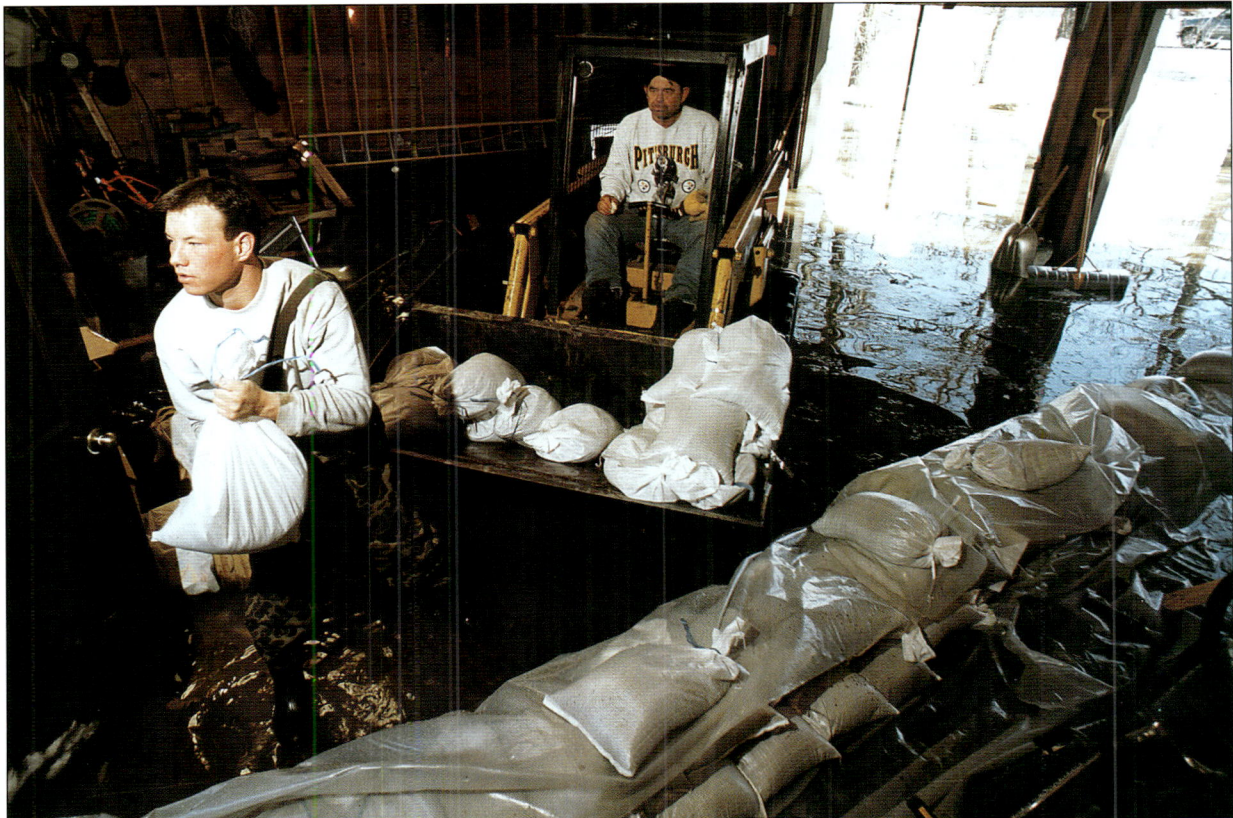

Daniel Parrow throws bags to other volunteers as his father runs a loader to help save their neighbor Ralph Lindstrom's home in Oakport Township. Diking through the garage, they ran pumps on the inside to flush water an inch from the top of Lindstrom's foundation. 87B

With this ring, I thee wet. Homes stand in water after sandbag ring dikes failed at the west end of 42nd Avenue South in Fargo. 88A

A Fargo city garbage truck doubles as a taxi as it carries 76 juniors and seniors from the school in Ulen-Hitterdal who came to Fargo to lend a hand in the flood-fighting effort. The students built a ring dike around a drain inlet with a malfunctioning valve that would have let in water from underneath a nearby dike that protects a condominium building along Elm Street near Mickelson Field. 88B

Working beneath the water level and behind a large dike made of sandbags and wood pallets braced by plenty of wood cross beams, Mark Dvoracek tacks plastic sheeting to the top of the structure protecting the home of Robert Hansen at 37 Woodland Drive in Fargo. 89A

"What wound will ever heal but by degrees?"
–William Shakespeare, *Othello*

IF NOT VICTORY, THERE IS HONOR

How tempting it is to resolve this tale in a satisfying turn of triumph. We like our stories to end that way. Especially the sad and scary ones.

We need to know that those so sorely abused by heartless fate and cruel circumstance are consoled and avenged in the final chapter. We sleep better when we close the book on characters who live happily ever after despite the tumult.

But life is not fairy-tale simple. And not even the winding Red River, master of switchbacks that it is, can twist so implausibly. Just as the river did not arrive happily at its end, neither can this story.

The wounds inflicted on the Valley by the blizzards and floods of 1996-97 were deep and many. They will be salved and stitched, and in time they will heal. But many will bear the scars for the rest of their days, and the ache of their loss may take decades to numb. To ignore that is to demean strain and suffering that came at a heavy price.

The financial injury to the region may exceed $2 billion. As they viewed the damage in the first days after the water subsided, leaders in the cities hardest hit vowed to rebuild their sacked infrastructure, their ruined schools, their hobbled churches and Main Streets.

At the same time, they feared an exodus of residents who had neither the emotional stamina nor the financial strength to take part in the renovation. For some, the simple act of waiting for recovery would become a luxury as self-indulgent and unaffordable as a two-carat diamond or a Mercedes Benz.

In its wake, the Red had unleashed a flood of uncertainty. How many farms and homes and businesses would never be reclaimed or replaced? As many as 20,000 people in Grand Forks alone lost their jobs overnight, so many that North Dakota's unemployment fund went searching for a federal bailout. How many would suffer financial ruin? What violence would it all do to the economy?

Talk arose that Grand Forks-East Grand Forks could lose as much as 25 percent of its combined population of 59,000 residents to Fargo and other cities with ready housing and work. A century from now, historians may point to the flood of '97 as the

ANDY BLENKUSH

Left: Members of the 4th Marine Division Reserve Unit sandbag plastic sheathing over an earthen dike in south Moorhead. 91A

Below: With shovels and boots muddy, volunteers pass an earthen dike under construction to protect a stretch of homes along Carrie Rose Lane in south Fargo near Rose Coulee. 91B

Facing page: Old Glory barely waves above the waves in the Lincoln Park area of Grand Forks. 90A

DAVE WALLIS

Looking southeast, not even a road is visible as water surrounds houses in the Timberline neighborhood in southwest Fargo. 92A

defining moment in the decline—or in the renaissance—of those stricken cities. Only time will tell which it will be.

The cost in tears and despair is far more difficult to tally.

How many years of history and human endeavor were washed and burned away? How many beautiful memories devoured? How much anguish endured? How many families collapsed beneath the weight of their troubles? How many lives disrupted and altered for the worse? There are no answers.

We like our stories to end in victory. We need to know that Rocky Balboa, cut and bruised and put bloody to the canvas, somehow finds his feet and rallies. But that did not happen. It never does in a battle against the elements. It's a fixed fight, you see. Nature always wins. Those are the rules.

Rocky lost. We lost.…

The words may not come without pain, but they come without shame. For though beaten, we fought well. And therein lies the greater glory.

Boundless courage and ingenuity stole round af-

ter round from an opponent who outweighed us, outsized us, and out-muscled us. It will never be known how many were spared misery and heartbreak and loss because of that unfailing refusal to submit.

"Our community fights like cats and dogs all year, but we are of one mind when the water comes up," Crookston's Floyd Spence boasted of his city.

The same can be echoed up and down the Valley where, when it mattered most, countless everyday heroes stood together, fell together, and helped each other stand again.

Author H. Jackson Brown Jr. observed that "Every person needs to have their moment in the sun, when they raise their arms in victory, knowing that on this day, at this hour, they were at their very best."

For the people of the Valley, that moment in the sun came many times in deepest night and bleakest day as they stood unflinchingly against the snow and the wind and the water.

And in the tempests we discovered—if not victory—then strength and honor in defeat.

Workers climb to the top of a huge dike of sandbags that protects the home of Sylvia Hove, 31 N.E. Woodland Drive, Fargo, from the rising Red River. On April 21, the concrete patio heaved, the west side of the dike started leaking and firefighters flooded the basement with clean water to avoid further damage. 93A

Dump trucks line up bumper-to-bumper as they hurry to build an emergency levee through expensive housing developments in southwest Fargo just before the crest. These trucks were dumping clay on 40th Avenue Southwest near Centennial Elementary School. 93B

National Guard trucks and boats crossed the moats and carried evacuees to safety at 4th Avenue and 6th Street North in Grand Forks. 94A

Ramona Skaurud, and her mother, Anna Balzum, struggle with emotion during a prayer service in Ada. 95A

Wake cottages. The Grand Forks Volunteer Water Rescue Team used personal watercraft to see that homes had been evacuated. 95B

This poster in the window of a Grand Forks city center business reflected the feeling of the community. 96A

A resident of the Riverside Park area in Grand Forks returns to his vehicle after making an initial assessment of his property's flooding. 96B

He ain't nothin' but a found dog. National Guardsman Tony Vondal emerges from the floodwaters in Grand Forks Saturday carrying a basset named "Trip" to safety. 97A COLBURN HVIDSTON III

> "By time and counsel do the best
> we can, the event is never in the
> power of man."
> —Robert Herrick, *Hesperides*

EPILOGUE

As the Red rumbled north from Grand Forks through the rest of the Valley, it displaced thousands more North Dakotans, Minnesotans and Canadians in towns along its banks.

In its wake came a bona fide traffic jam of trucks bearing food, clothes and supplies, gifts from a generous nation. Money poured too as countless people emptied their pockets. One benefactor—a woman who for a while would be known only as Angel—pledged $2,000 to most every flood-stricken household in Grand Forks and East Grand Forks. She would later be identified as McDonald's heiress Joan Kroc. "It's like getting $2,000 hugs," wept one grateful woman after she received her check. The total gift could amount to more than $15 million. A second anonymous benefactor donated another $5 million.

In the months and years to follow, the Flood of '97 will be analyzed from every conceivable angle. What went right? What went wrong? Who's to credit? Who's to blame?

Given the repeated failings of flood gauges and crest forecasts, questions will be raised about our ability—or lack thereof—to predict the rise and fall of the river accurately.

Old debates about the need for drainage, the supply and necessity of wetlands, and the folly of building in the flood plain no doubt will rekindle.

"Why build up for a repeat performance?" asks Paul Suomala of the International Coalition For Land and Water Stewardship in the Red River Valley. "Shouldn't there be some basin-wide zoning standards?"

The Red River Basin Board—composed of members from North and South Dakota, Minnesota, and Manitoba—could consider the question along with others concerning the development of wetlands and man-made flood controls.

"We need a comprehensive water management plan that includes water supply, quality and flood prevention," said Moorhead Mayor Morris Lanning, who is a member of the basin board. "This is simply something we must do."

It is a worthy pursuit. Answering the myriad questions posed by the Flood of '97 may help avert future calamity.

At the same time we will do well to remember our limits. In the words of Napoleon Hill: "Nature cannot be tricked or cheated. She will give up to you the object of your struggles only after you have paid her price."

The price of living in the Red River Valley is regular flooding. And it will be so as long as the Valley is flat and snow settles on its fields.

The south side of Breckenridge is swamped by breakout water from the Bois de Sioux River. It was the second attack of flooding for the beleaguered city.
98-99A

Right: Milton Dahlstad evicts the river from his basement in Ada and bids the unwanted tenant good riddance. 100A

Below: After the floodwaters ebbed away, cleanup began in Ada. 100B

Shall we gather at the river? Fortunately not. Floodwaters did not invade the sanctuary of historic St. Michael's Catholic Church in Grand Forks. 101A

Pitching in. Paul Myers, left, and Lt. Kevin Cedervall unload a truck of much-needed supplies at a relocation center at the United Methodist Church in Breckenridge. 102A

BRUCE CRUMMY

Left: Cleanup tasks in Ada were un-pleasant to say the least. Worker Mike Longworth hauls one of several loads of spoiled athletic apparel from the basement of Ada-Borup High School. 103A

Below: A National Guard Humvee rolls through the water at 5th Street South and Oregon Avenue in Breckenridge. 103B

NICK CARLSON

Above: Flood victim Nancy Edwards struggles to hold back tears during an all-faiths prayer service in Ada. "You have been violated terribly," the Rev. Karl Schmidt told the 200 flood victims gathered for the first time since the city was inundated. 104A

Right: Sheets of broken ice, remnants of the flood that ravaged Ada, are spread throughout the town as the cleanup begins. 104-105A

No rest for the flood-weary. John Seedorf loads a mattress into a truck at Slim's Home Furnishings in Breckenridge. The store's showroom was flooded. 106A

Members of the Valley Water Rescue Team assist in securing plastic sheeting over a massive earthen dike in south Moorhead. 106B

Paul Ames surveys the wreckage in the basement at his home just off Highway 81 south of Fargo. 107A

A second earthen levee protected Fargo City Hall and Civic Auditorium and other downtown properties should the dike on Second Street, at left in photo, fail. The dike on Third Street North was built after a leak was found in the primary dike and patched with clay.   108-109A DAVE WALLIS

ACKNOWLEDGMENTS

It's funny about covering spring floods. You know when rivers will rise, how high and roughly how much land will be flooded. But that's only the starting blocks for newspaper street-people. Photographers and reporters learn it's hard work wading through waist-high floodwater while wearing hip boots just to get to one site…that flooded streets have a current that can sweep you away…that the top of a dike is no place to tarry…that covering the human misery of a flood is as emotionally draining as it is physically tiring.

Reporters stare at keyboards trying to find another word to replace "sandbag" or "blizzard"; photographers move to another position so tomorrow's photo won't look like today's knowing they'll have the same problem tomorrow.

The term "long hours" takes on a whole new meaning. So do words. Like tragedy. Disaster. Volunteer.

But these are strange birds, these newspaper street-people. They don't want to take a day off when they're the messengers of something special. When finally they are forced to rest for a day, many return to the scene as caring citizens to help with a resident's dike or fill sandbags.

It took almost everybody in our newsroom to cover the five months of blizzards and floods.

Copy editors, graphic artists and opinion page staff involved were Rob Beer, Dawn Brehm, Mark Merck, Trygve Olson, Helmut Schmidt, Patrick Spaeth, Steve Stark, Doug Tweed, Jay Ulku, Matt Von Pinnon, Roger Whittle and Jack Zaleski.

Senior editors and department heads directing coverage were John Lohman, Terry DeVine, Dennis Doeden, David Jurgens and Cathy Zaiser.

Reporters—the foot soldiers for the long winter and spring—were Patrick Condon, Ellen Crawford, Deneen Gilmour, Gerry Gilmour, DeAnne Hilgers, Jon Knutson, David Kolpack, Bob Lind, Craig McEwen, David Olson, Tom Pantera, Mikkel Pates, Karyn Spencer, Jack Sullivan, John Sundvor and Tammy Swift.

The material for this book was assembled from their stories and written by fellow reporter Christopher Sprung.

Page 112: The fickle Red River corkscrews its way north to Manitoba's Lake Winnipeg. 112A LARRY MAYER

Forum photo staffers: From left, Dave Wallis, Colburn Hvidston III, Bruce Crummy, Andy Blenkush, Nick Carlson.

Larry Mayer

Christopher Sprung